D0827958

How to Raise a Reader

Other books by Elaine K. McEwan

Leading Your Team to Excellence: How to Make Quality Decisions

Seven Steps to Effective Instructional Leadership

The Principal's Guide to Attention Deficit Disorder

The Principal's Guide to Raising Reading Achievement

Counseling Tips for the Elementary School Principal (with Jeffrey Kottler)

Managing Unmanageable Students: Positive Solutions for Administrators (with Mary Damer)

Solving School Problems: Kindergarten through Middle School

ABC's of School Success

Attention Deficit Disorder

"Nobody Likes Me" Helping Your Child Make Freinds

"I Didn't Do It" Dealing with Dishonesty

"Mom, He Hit Me!" What to Do about Sibling Rivalry

"The Dog Ate It" Conquering Homework Hassles

Managing Attention and Learning Disorders: A Guide for Adults

When Kids Say NO to School: Helping Children at Risk of Failure, Refusal, or Dropping Out

Angry Parents, Failing Schools: What's Wrong with the Public Schools and What You Can Do About It

Top Ten Traits of a Highly Successful School: How Can You Tell if Your School is a Good One?

How to Raise a Reader

• • •

Elaine K. McEwan

Baker Books

A Division of Baker Book House Co
Grand Rapids, Michigan 49516

© 1999 by Elaine K. McEwan

Published by Baker Books
a division of Baker Book House Company
P.O. Box 6287, Grand Rapids, MI 49516-6287

Printed in the United States of America

All rights reserved. No part of this publication may be reproduced, stored in a retrieval system, or transmitted in any form or by any means—for example, electronic, photocopy, recording—without the prior written permission of the publisher. The only exception is brief quotations in printed reviews.

Library of Congress Cataloging-in-Publication Data

McEwan, Elaine K., 1941–
    How to raise a reader / Elaine K. McEwan.
        p.   cm.
    Includes bibliographical references and indexes.
    ISBN 0-8010-1184-1 (paper)
    1. Reading—Parent participation—United States. 2. Children—Books and reading—United States. 3. Children—Books and reading—United States Bibliography. 4. Children's literature, English Bibiography. I. Title.
    LB1050.2.M374   1999
    649'.58—dc21   99-22613

Scripture is from the Revised Standard Version of the Bible, copyright 1946, 1952, 1971 by the Division of Christian Education of the National Council of the Churches of Christ in the USA. Used by permission.

For current information about all releases from Baker Book House, visit our web site:
                    http://www.bakerbooks.com

Contents

• • •

Contents

I Learned to Read Today

• • •

You may have tangible wealth untold:
Caskets of jewels and coffers of gold.
Richer than I you can never be—
I had a Mother who read to me.

Strickland Gillilan

When my first child went off to kindergarten, I experienced all of the usual emotions. Not only was she leaving the nest, but in those new surroundings she would be instructed, examined, and evaluated. Would she measure up? Would she have fun? Would she like school? And most important to me, would she learn to read? I already knew my daughter liked books; I read aloud to her daily. I also knew that she understood and remembered a great deal of what we read together. But I had no idea if she could or even would learn to read with ease. My earlier attempts at teaching her had not been notable. Consequently I didn't even attempt to teach her to read. I decided ful experience we shared with books was too special to risk turning it into a battle.

She went off to kindergarten with anticipation and was not disappointed. One day in early October, she arrived home to announce, "I learned to read today." I couldn't believe what I was hearing. Perhaps she had confused writing letters on paper with reading. "Can you read for me?" I asked her with barely contained excitement. To this point she had never read a single word aloud to me. Eagerly I pulled out a library book she had never seen before. She promptly began reading aloud with fluency and expression as if this were something we had been doing regularly.

In actuality reading aloud was something we had been doing regularly. Only now the roles were reversed. My child was reading to me. And I realized that in her mind, she had learned to read in one day at school. She was not yet aware that the preparation for this moment had been five years of continuing conversation, incessant questions, endless repetitions of nursery rhymes and poems, and the reading aloud of hundreds of her favorite picture books.

Reading aloud is the single most important thing that parents can do to ensure school success for their children. But, lest you think that every child will learn to read exactly like Emily did, let me assure you that is not the case.

In my relative naïveté as a parent I fully expected my daughter's story to repeat itself when I sent my son, Patrick, off to kindergarten two years later. After all, he had experienced five years of the same reading-rich environment, would attend the very same school, and would have the same teacher. I had no reason to think that his experiences with reading would be any different than his sister's. He was a bright and eager learner. October came and went, however, and he didn't come home to tell me he had learned to read. He learned his sounds and began to blend simple words but he never read aloud to me with fluency as his sister had done. In first grade he completed a phonics program as part of the basal reading series. We continued to read aloud every night. He read to me from simple readers, sounding out each word carefully, experiencing success every step of the way, and slowly developing the fluency and automaticity that comes from successful repeated practice. In second grade the final pieces of the reading puzzle fell into place for him and he truly began to read. Over one thousand books, actually. By spring he was reading full-length novels by E. B. White and Beverly Cleary.

Patrick needed structured phonics instruction in kindergarten and first grade to help him put together the reading puzzle for himself. Although his smooth and steady progression toward becoming a successful reader was based on the critical foundation of five years of continuing conversation, incessant questions, endless repetitions of nursery rhymes and poems, and the reading aloud of hundreds of his favorite picture books, Patrick needed an additional boost— effective reading instruction—to help him acquire the tools of decoding, an essential skill for all readers.

Emily and Patrick are grown up now; they are both avid readers and excellent writers. I know that the heritage of their grandparents—who read aloud to their parents—and their parents—who read aloud to them—will be repeated once again when they have families of their own. And I hope that you'll want to begin reading aloud to your children as soon as you can find a good book to share. If you have questions about how to begin, you'll find answers to your questions and suggestions for the best books to read in the pages ahead.

What Is Reading?

Reading is a complex cognitive process. First, the reader needs to translate the letters (symbols) on the printed page into sounds that can be blended into recognizable words. Then he needs to identify the meaning of each word that is read and create a visual image or concept of it. Finally, all of the words in a sentence or paragraph must come together to create a main idea or story for the reader that can be comprehended, retold, and remembered. The reader (whether child or adult) needs to understand, react, and learn from the printed page in order to really be reading. Mere word calling—pronunciation without comprehension—is not reading. One must know the code that enables him to unlock the pronunciation of a new word and then be able to recognize (or find out) what the word means in the context of the written passage.

For beginning readers, this process is often painstaking and highly visible to the observer, somewhat like watching a child learn to ride a bicycle. One can almost feel the "mental wheels" turn in unison with the bicycle wheels as the novice rider deals with the multiple tasks of remaining balanced while at the same time steering, braking, and avoiding obstacles in the path. With practice, the new rider gains fluency, automaticity, and can even enjoy the scenery or steer with one hand. A similar process occurs in reading; a child moves from slow, careful decoding and step-by-step thinking to processing hundreds of words with fluency, remarkable speed, understanding, and enjoyment. The process seems effortless and is scarcely noticeable when done well. The head moves, the eyes blink, and the pages turn; another child has been introduced to the wonder of the printed page.

For those who prefer a formal definition of reading, this is my favorite: "the meaningful interpretation of printed or written verbal symbols."[1] The key words in this definition are "meaningful interpretation." For reading to take place, the reader must gain meaning.

Why Is Reading So Important?

When I was an elementary school principal I asked a group of kindergarten parents at an orientation meeting what they wanted their children to learn during the school year. The majority answered: "To read." Success in school at any level is based on reading ability. A child's self-concept as a student is frequently centered in his earliest experiences with learning to read. Our testing programs are based on the ability to read. Most important, reading is our link with the world. We can share ideas, travel, learn, experience the pain and joy of others, and enrich our lives. Lifelong learning is made difficult, if not impossible, when an individual is not a skilled reader.

Illiteracy is one of our country's biggest social problems. The United States Department of Education estimates that twenty-seven million Americans can't decipher a street sign or the number on a bus and forty-five million have never read a book or newspaper. These people are cut off from jobs, family, and the ability to learn and grow as human beings.

How Do Children Learn to Read?

How children learn to read has been the subject of controversy for decades, but particularly during the past fifteen years. Unfortunately this debate between two groups of researchers and educators, those who espouse a philosophy called "whole language" and those in a camp known as "phonics," has resulted in more than a generation of schoolchildren losing out on some critical teaching essential to learning to read. (If you are interested in learning more about phonics versus whole language, consult resource A.) Either philosophy practiced in isolation deprives children of experiences that are critical to being literate adults. The whole-language folks believe that all children will learn to read naturally, developmentally, just as they learn to talk and walk. Simply immersing children in good books is all that is necessary to produce fluent and capable readers. They make fun of the "drill and kill" of phonics and tell parents not to worry if a child isn't reading by third grade.

In fairness, whole-language teachers and researchers have made all educators and parents more aware of the importance of immersing children in outstanding children's literature before, during, and after formal reading instruction as well as the critical importance of "print awareness." Print awareness includes knowing the purpose of reading (getting meaning and understanding from the printed text); how stories work (they usually have characters, a setting, and a plot); how words are composed of letters and what spaces signify; and directionality (how print is organized, which necessitates the ability to scan left to right and then sweep diagonally left and one line down).[2] Perhaps if I had raised only my first child and had not been an educator myself, I might have been seduced by the lovely but very naive notion of whole language—that all children learn to read naturally.

The phonics folks, on the other hand, believe that all a child needs to become a fluent reader is a healthy dose of phonics in kindergarten and/or first grade. Expose a child to a sequential and explicit phonics program that teaches the alphabetic code and how it works to represent speech and he will automatically become a fluent reader, they say; give a child intensive instruction and practice in how to sound out words rather than reading them as a whole or guessing and he'll be reading in no time. I could just as easily have been taken in by the belief that phonics was the only answer for every child. After all, it worked just fine for my son, Patrick, and for many other children with whom I've worked.

On the job as principal of a large, very diverse elementary school in the suburbs of Chicago, I saw a third group of children: those who hadn't come to school already knowing how to read and who didn't respond to the excellent "phonics first" instruction they were given, either. For these students remedial reading was often the first stop on a route that was headed straight for school failure. What was the missing piece of their reading puzzle?

Researchers have always known that some children learned to read with ease no matter what methodology was used to teach them, while others struggled or failed, even when they were taught with an explicit, systematic phonics program. The mystery of just why this happened has only recently begun to unfold.[3] Researchers have identified and described a set of critical skills that were missing in children who had severe reading difficulties. This set of understandings that every child must have before he can learn to read is called phonemic (or phonological) awareness. Phonemic awareness concerns the most basic element of the language system, the phoneme (an individual sound). This awareness consists of the ability to recognize individual sounds in words and leads to the ability to rhyme, blend spoken sounds into words, and count phonemes. Lack of phonemic awareness in kindergarten or first grade is an almost certain indicator that a child will have future reading problems.[4]

Phonemic awareness is the first building block in the reading process. There are three ways that children acquire phonemic awareness: (1) genetically, by being born with strong phonemic awareness abilities; (2) from environmental influences, through reading aloud and language development activities from birth to age six; and (3) through explicit instruction, by being taught from a systematic program at school age.

Consider young people who are gifted athletes. Many have a strong genetic background; their parents are good athletes, even stars. But these parents don't rely on genetics alone to raise a tennis player or a football star. They don't wait to see if a star has been born; they engage in all kinds of activities that build athletic awareness from birth. A recent young golf phenomenon, Tiger Woods, is pictured swinging a golf club when he was just a toddler. Explicit instruction in the rules and finer points of the game can wait until a child is older, but hundreds of hours of awareness activities build a strong foundation and create a desire and readiness in the child to n how to play the game like the grown-ups do. The process works the same way if you want to raise a reader.

If you want your child to love reading and be a good reader, don't spend even a minute worrying about genetics. It's something over which you have absolutely no control. Focus on what you do have control over—the phonemic awareness and reading readiness activities that you can give to your child by sharing good books. To raise a reader, read aloud to your child every day from the day of his birth. Have a wide range of printed materials available in your home. Give your children paper, pencils, chalk, chalkboards, markers, and magnetic letters. Respond to all of your child's attempts to make sense of the printed word and to produce "writing" on his own. Let your child know that you value reading, and demonstrate your feelings by reading yourself. Let your child know that you expect him to be a successful reader and that you will do all in your power to help him. In addition to sharing books with your child, share dinner table conversation and have bedtime chats. Every language experience you have with your child is like money in his "school bank."

How Can I Help My Child Develop Print and Phonemic Awareness?

Although the skills of print and phonemic awareness sound simple enough—knowing how print operates and knowing that our language is made up of sounds—the lack of this learning stands in the way of hundreds of thousands of children learning to read every year. How can such simple things be missing from so many children's life experiences? The answer is also very simple: No one took the time to read aloud and talk to them every day.

Phonemic awareness has a natural progression that you can follow as you choose books to read aloud to your child.

1. Begin with nursery rhymes, chants, fingerplays, and songs to develop your child's ability to recognize pairs of rhyming words or to produce his own sets of words that rhyme. There is nothing quite so delightful as having fun with silly games and rhymes, meanwhile knowing that you are giving your child the precious gift of reading.

2. Use alphabet books to have fun with what are called "sound-oddity tasks," the ability to identify words that are the same or different in terms of beginning, middle, or ending sounds.

3. Use simple books that feature photographs or drawings of real objects with single words on a page, to demonstrate blending tasks (the ability to pronounce syllables or phonemes separately and then combine them into identifiable words). As your child becomes more aware of the relationship between the spoken word and the printed word, point to the words as you read them.

Chapter 3 contains a recommended list of rhyming books for developing phonemic awareness. If you are interested in a more comprehensive discussion of phonemic awareness as well as specific activities to use with your child, I highly recommend the book *Phonemic Awareness in Young Children*.[5] Also check out resource B for recommended materials to teach phonemic awareness at home or school as well as assessments that parents and professionals can use to determine if a phonemic awareness deficit may be standing in the way of reading success.

What If There Isn't Enough Time to Read Aloud to My Child?

You're not alone in your frustration over the time crunch in your life. Lack of time plus the pressures of having more than one child are the top two reasons parents don't read more to their offspring. But some parents just don't realize how important reading aloud actually is. A 1996 study done for the Reading Is Fundamental program found that only 50 percent of the 525 parents of two to eight year olds polled in the study read to their children daily—for about twenty minutes.[6] Ruth Graves, head of RIF, speculated that many parents, particularly more affluent parents, may be taking for granted that their children will grow up to be readers. If you had to answer the survey questions about how often you read aloud to your children, what would your answer be?

One of the most effective kindergarten teachers I ever encountered in my career as an elementary school principal developed a very compelling technique to encourage those parents who otherwise might have been tempted to forget reading aloud. Her method was somewhat similar to the way commercials persuade parents to buy sugar-coated cereals. She used the children as leverage.

Children returned a signed slip for each book their parents had read aloud. When they turned in the slips to their teacher, the children received stars on a chart. When they acquired a certain number of stars, they received a certificate. Soon every child was begging his parents to read aloud to him every night. I only wish all children were born beseeching their parents to read aloud to them. I wish every newborn came with the following instructions for parents: "For optimum development, please read aloud to me every day beginning today. Recite nursery rhymes and poems and expose me to all of the classics of children's literature. There is nothing you can do for me that will be more important to my school success."

I cannot state my case with any more urgency. I am begging you to read aloud to your child as regularly and as often as you can. It is as important as daily teeth brushing. I have laughingly joked with parents that we have all the technology necessary to repair teeth; repairing reading problems is a far more complex task. If you don't spend time reading aloud during your child's early years, you'll pay the price when your child heads off to school. Don't count on the schools to make up the deficits! Some children will never catch up if they start school too far behind their peers.

There are ways to find the time to read aloud. How about the waiting room at the doctor's office? Use the moments while you're waiting for that long freight train. When you're dying to put your feet up and the kids won't leave you alone, read. Whenever you've run out of entertainment ideas, try a book. One of our favorite times was just before bed. I could almost feel the tension leave our bodies and minds as we quietly read aloud one of our favorites like *Good Night Moon* or *Bedtime for Frances*. Reading aloud is a wonderful transition between an active day and your child's willing trip off to bed.

Shouldn't Reading Instruction Be Left to Trained Teachers in the Schools?

You cannot depend on the schools to teach phonemic awareness (the first step to reading) and after that phonics (the next step) to your child. Many classroom teachers still subscribe to the whole-language philosophy that believes all children will learn to read naturally without explicit, systematic instruction in either phonemic awareness or phonics. Even if your child is fortunate enough to attend a school where both phonemic awareness and phonics are included in the kindergarten and first-grade curricula, he will still have missed all of the shared experiences, background, and knowledge he could bring to formal instruction if you had begun reading aloud to him in infancy. You can never bring back those precious years with their enormous potential for learning once they are gone.

Dr. Burton J. White, a respected physician and researcher at Harvard University in the field of child development, says, "Relatively few families, perhaps no more than 10 percent, manage to get their children through the eight to thirty-six month age period as well educated and developed as they can and should be."[7] There is enormous potential for informal learning that exists in the home through parent-child interaction.

You don't need degrees and diplomas. You don't need the trappings of technology. You don't need to be remarkably learned about education and psychology. You only need a remarkable respect for the mind of a child, a willingness to be consistent, lots of patience, and hundreds of good books. Do not make the mistake of believing that computer games, videos, and television programs will substitute for reading aloud. They can never take the place of one-to-one adult-child experiences with books.

Chapter 2 contains some specific suggestions for just how you can establish the read aloud tradition in your home. If your children are older, check out chapter 9, "Seventy-Plus Ways to Raise a Reader." The list contains some excellent suggestions for beginning the read aloud habit, even if you're getting a late start.

Read It One More Time, Daddy

• • •

It was two or three years ago—I can't remember which—that she came to me, crawled upon my lap dragging behind her a dog-eared book of pages smeared with magic words and peanut butter, and suggested (she didn't implore or beg or demand, but she suggested), "Help me read it, Daddy; help me read it."

She is gone now; married with a child of her own, so she doesn't come anymore to sit on my lap. But she does call on the telephone and suggests, "Help me read it, Daddy. Help me read it."

Cliff Schimmels

My husband was raised in the city. I was raised in the country. His family always planted a garden on their thirty-foot lot. My family bought all of its produce at my father's grocery store. My husband's family took summer vacations in different places. We always stayed at home because my dad had to tend to the store. Despite our differences, however, we did find a common thread running through our childhoods—the importance to our families of reading.

There were always books, newspapers, and magazines strewn about the house in spite of my mother's high housekeeping standards. She read Sunday school manuals, her well-worn Bible, and devotional books, while my father read trade magazines, theology books, and newspapers. In my husband's family, reading tastes ran to poetry, history, and the classics. But our families both agreed that reading was important.

I have memories of my mother reading aloud to comfort and quiet me when I had the measles, memories of bicycling over two miles each week to the bookmobile that visited our rural area, and memories of gliding back and forth on the porch swing while curled up with a scary mystery. My husband remembers his father telling folktales and adventure stories of the sea, he remembers making the difficult decision about which fourteen books he would choose from the public library to take along on his summer vacation, and he remembers swinging on a porch swing similar to mine while reading a spine-tingling adventure story.

When we talked about becoming parents, we always mentioned creating those same warm feelings and good memories about books and reading for our children. We began to purchase children's books even before we had children.

If you have a desire to raise readers as we did and have questions about how to begin, this chapter will answer many of those questions. You will find out why reading aloud is one of the most important shared experiences you can have with your children, when and how you should begin reading aloud, and how to choose appropriate materials to read aloud.

What Is Reading Aloud?

Perhaps you're wondering why we even need to define reading aloud. But the dismal statistics regarding illiteracy, drop-out rates, and enrollments in remedial reading classes show that for many people, reading aloud has been an uncommon experience.

Reading aloud is a shared experience in which one person reads a story or entire book to another person or group. Reading aloud takes place in church each Sunday as the minister or lector reads the lessons of the day to the congregation. Reading aloud takes place in thousands of school classrooms as teachers read to students. And reading aloud takes place each time a parent puts a child on her lap and makes a story come to life.

What Are the Benefits of Reading Aloud?

Books have a marvelous capacity for helping adults build relationships with children. Reading a book together gives adult and child a shared background and experience. When my children and I see a spider building a web in the corner of a room, we immediately think of Charlotte, that famous spider from E. B. White's classic, *Charlotte's Web*. When we have breaded veal cutlets for dinner, our family shares a moment of fun singing Frances's song about what veal cutlets wear before they're breaded from the delightful story *Bread and Jam for Frances*.

When the significant adults in a child's life are willing to spend time cuddled in a rocking chair or snuggled on a couch, an unmistakable message is sent: "I love you and I care enough about you to spend time with you." When you are reading aloud to a child, she has your undivided attention, a rare occurrence in our fast-paced, dual-career world. When you are willing at any moment to lay aside your pressing concerns and share a read-aloud, your child experiences an inner glow that she'll be able to recall even when she's grown.

Reading aloud gives the child an understanding of the purpose of the printed word and a growing familiarity with written language that is essential to successful reading in school. Children who begin their school careers with hundreds of hours of read-alouds behind them will have an advantage that can never be reclaimed for children who have been deprived of those experiences. Researcher Keith Stanovich has labeled this advantage the "Matthew effect"[1] based on the New Testament parable of the talents in which the rich get richer and the poor get poorer: "For to every one who has will more be given, and he will have abundance; but from him who has not, even what he has will be taken away" (Matt. 25:29 RSV). Students who have experienced a rich read aloud environment will be blessed with advantages that will multiply for them during their school careers. Those children for whom reading aloud has not been a daily experience may never make up the deficits.

My daughter, Emily, took a driver's training course the summer she turned sixteen. Getting her ready to drive a car had not been high on our list of priorities during the year. Her father knew that he didn't have the patience. I just hadn't had the time. Therefore she entered the class with no hands-on experience.

She came home after the first class and said her teacher was astounded that she had never driven a car before. "How did you reach the age of sixteen without ever starting or steering a car?" he wanted to know. Other members of her driving group already knew how to drive. The teacher would only fine-tune their skills and give them the credential they needed.

Many parents are not willing to entrust their student driver's education to the schools. They want to be involved. I wonder if these same parents had an equal concern for their child's readiness for reading before she started kindergarten. Fortunately, we were able to bring Emily up to speed behind the wheel of a car with a daily tutorial in the parking lot of a local industrial park. Recovering deficits in reading is not that simple, however.

Consider what a five year old who has not had a daily read aloud experience with parents and other caregivers might experience if she starts school with classmates who have been exposed to books since birth. Think about what your child might feel if she realizes her peers already understand the rules of the spoken and written word and she doesn't.

Young children have an enormous capacity for learning. Reading a wide variety of books will give them a chance to learn about human emotions, people, places, and Bible stories, plus trucks, trains, and animals. The list is endless. In addition, reading aloud will help your child develop the ability to build mental images of the printed word, a critical skill that is fast becoming extinct because of the proliferation of television, videos, and computer games. With vivid mental pictures of the words they hear and read, proficient readers are able to understand and remember what they read.

For parents there are four principal reasons for reading aloud. First, and most important, reading aloud will bring the delights of developing a close relationship with your child and build memories that will last a lifetime. Second, exposing your child to classics plus the best in new books for children will encourage your child to be a voracious reader, a good writer, and an individual with creativity and imagination. Third, reading from the best in nonfiction and concept books will help your child acquire a vast storehouse of knowledge and information about the world. Finally, reading aloud from the best in children's literature will expose your children to important virtues and values—teaching her lessons of faith, courage, love, honesty, and loyalty that will last for a lifetime.

Who Should Read Aloud?

Is reading aloud so difficult and important that only specially trained people can do it? Of course not. Each one of a child's primary caregivers should read aloud regularly to the child and should ensure the child is being read to faithfully by baby-sitters, day-care providers, and preschools.

When my children were three and five, I took a part-time summer position as a school librarian. My children needed care while I was away, and so I hired an energetic high school student with excellent references. I was gone for only three hours each day, but I helped her put together a schedule that would keep the children busy and happy—a little water play in the wading pool, a walk to the local park, a snack on the patio, riding Big Wheels on the driveway, and of course reading aloud several stories. I carried armloads of books home from the library where I was working.

When I returned from my work each day, I talked with the children to find out what they had been doing. One part of the schedule never seemed to be completed—reading aloud. I mentioned it to the baby-sitter on more than one occasion. She always smiled and nodded. But somehow the stories never got read. Although she followed all of my other instructions to the letter, I soon realized that Joan wasn't going to read the stories. I didn't pressure her or embarrass her in front of my children. The summer job was soon over and I didn't ask Joan to return. I wanted anyone who spent time with my children to read aloud to them.

Fathers should most definitely be included in the group of primary caregivers we mentioned earlier. All of the shared experiences shouldn't just be between Mom and the kids. My favorite snapshot (which I've since had rendered as a portrait) shows my husband snuggled up in our big leather chair reading *Davy and His Dog* to a freshly bathed and ready-for-bed fourteen month old. She is pointing to the dog and seems to be saying, "Read it again, Daddy. Read it again." The hours that Emily and Patrick shared in read-alouds with their father are even more precious to them since his death in 1990.

Older brothers and sisters can read to younger children also. Grandparents and aunts and uncles can be enlisted. Baby-sitters should always read aloud. And, of course, teachers should read aloud too.

When Should I Begin Reading Aloud?

The minute I found out we were expecting our first child, I began reading books about pregnancy, child care, and child development. I read everything our public library had available. One book in particular intrigued me. It was titled *How to Raise a Brighter Child*.[2] Some of the ideas were new; some were controversial. Researchers were just beginning to find out that the period from birth to three years was crucial in terms of development. The book emphasized the importance of treating your infant as a person from the very beginning, talking and reading to her.

When Emily wouldn't sleep in the middle of the night, I held her in the rocking chair while reciting poems and nursery rhymes, singing songs, and telling her Bible stories. Those storytelling sessions got me through many sleepless nights. When she was six months old, I began reading to her from easy books. I talked nonstop. Shoppers would look at me strangely in the grocery store while I carried on a seemingly one-sided conversation with an infant, but I chattered on.

Begin reciting poems, rhymes, and songs from the very beginning. Then begin reading simple stories to your baby. Don't make the mistake of thinking that just because your infant isn't responding in some way that she is not learning.

Where Should I Read Aloud?

The wonderful thing about books is their portability. When my children were small I always carried several books in the car. The Chicago suburb in which we lived was divided into north and south by railroad tracks. Commuter trains roared by several times each hour, and frequent mile-long freight trains created massive traffic backups. We often read while waiting for the trains to go by. Reading aloud has a wonderful way of calming restless children. You can read anywhere you have to wait with children.

Choose a comfortable location in your home and designate it as the read aloud corner. An overstuffed chair, if you're reading to just one child, is the perfect spot. Or perhaps the heirloom rocking chair in the nursery. When you're reading to two children, you'll need a cozy couch. Where you read aloud, although all participants should be comfortable, is not nearly as important as the fact that you are doing it.

How Often Should I Read Aloud?

When children are very small, we have to read aloud when they are receptive and ready, not necessarily on our own timetable. But very soon, habits will be formed and they will learn to expect stories every day, as regularly as they expect their meals. Those of you who are flexible, easygoing, unplanned, and spontaneous will need to concentrate on making sure that reading aloud occurs with regularity every day. Those of you who are programmed, structured, planned, and organized will need to work on meeting your child's needs for flexibility. You should not attempt to program reading aloud when your child has other needs or interests.

How Long Should the Read Aloud Session Be?

We must be sensitive to the developmental stages and individual needs of our children. I have often seen hysterical children being dragged through shopping centers during the late evening hours. I know their behavior is not because they are bad children. Their parents simply haven't tuned in to their needs for early bedtime or possibly a snack break.

The same principle applies to the read aloud sessions. Capitalize on every quiet moment you can with your active toddler or preschooler. If she's ready for a story, be prepared to drop what you're doing and respond. Don't force a child to sit and listen when she's scrambling off your lap. <u>Don't turn reading aloud into a battle of wills. Five or six minutes of quiet reading may be the maximum in the beginning</u>. As children's attention spans increase and their interests mature, you can stretch this time. Be prepared, however, for those children who will listen to as many stories at bedtime as you are willing to read.

What Should I Read Aloud?

The most delightful task of parenting is the fun of exploring the wonderful world of children's literature and choosing from the thousands of available books those that you will share with your child. While preparing to be an elementary school teacher I took a course in children's literature at Wheaton College. Dr. Roger Shuy was the teacher and he made children's books come alive for me. While earning my degree in library science, I took more courses in children's literature. But reading children's books to fulfill academic requirements was not nearly as rewarding as reading them to real children, my own and the hundreds who have passed through my school libraries and classrooms. <u>Only as books are read aloud can one begin to appreciate what is really appropriate in a read-aloud</u>.

Choosing children's books is not a science. Selection is a very personal matter. However, if you're brand new at choosing books to read aloud, chapters 3, 4, and 5 include dozens of suggestions. All of the books included have been personally field-tested for their readability and carefully examined to be age and content appropriate. Here are two simple guidelines to use in choosing books.

- Choose books that you like. If you don't like a story, you will obviously have a difficult time reading it aloud with enthusiasm and enjoyment. Your opinion counts!
- Choose books that interest your child. These interests will become evident as your child grows older. Does she clap with delight whenever you encounter a cat on your walk through the neighborhood? Why not read *Angus and the Cat* by Marjorie Flack? Buy your own copy of that classic *Spot the Dog* by Eric Hill if your preschooler loves to get involved in what she is reading. She can lift the tabs on each page to try to find the missing puppy.

You can afford to be less rigid in your selection standards if you are borrowing books from a library, since any mistakes you make in choosing need only be returned on the next visit. When you begin to purchase books (especially hardcover) for your child's personal library, make sure that you buy with care. There are many excellent reading lists compiled by other authors in addition to my suggestions. See resource C for a complete list of titles.

The children's book publishing industry annually awards prestigious prizes for the best in children's illustrations—the Caldecott Medal—and the best in children's writing—the Newberry Medal. In addition to giving a first prize in each category, several runners-up are chosen, designated as honor books. Often a local bookstore or public library will publish a list of the winners each year, and the reference librarian at your public library can point you to books that contain a complete listing of all prizewinners and honor books.

There is much debate among parents, librarians, and educators each year as to the worthiness of the selections. Many of the contemporary titles chosen for the Newberry Medal contain themes and language that are objectionable to some, and this trend shows no sign of abating. Even an occasional Caldecott Medal book will raise questions with regard to subject matter. As a parent, you must carefully consider how you will spend your child's time and your book dollar.

Where Can I Get Books to Read Aloud to My Child?

Bookstores (used and new), supermarkets, swap stores, wholesale clubs, libraries, book clubs, garage sales, and friends whose children are grown—books are available everywhere these days. It's a good thing they are so plentiful, because when your children get into the read aloud habit, you'll need an ample supply. The public library will always provide the variety and quantity needed to keep even the most prolific read aloud families supplied, paid for by your tax dollars, of course. Make sure that every member of your family has a library card. Perhaps your local school library is open for parental check-out as well. Many school libraries offer summer hours and reading programs for both parents and children.

However, don't overlook the joy your child will receive from having her own books to read whenever she chooses. We always bought hardcover editions of our favorites, knowing that these would be treasured and read aloud to our children's children and their children. Begin now to build your own home library with some of the selections from the following chapters.

What Do I Do First?

Sometimes new parents feel awkward and embarrassed about reciting poetry and nursery rhymes or talking with a very young child, but your child is listening, and as you sense your child's growing interest and enthusiasm for reading

ou'll soon lose your apprehension. Here are some
uidelines to get you started with your newborn.

- Begin with easy board books that contain single pictures of familiar animals and people in everyday situations. Point at the clothes, details, and colors of the pictures. Be enthusiastic and dramatic in your reading.

- Graduate to books that show animals and people doing things or as characters in simple stories.

- Talk about what is happening now, what happened earlier, and what might happen next in the stories you read. These are important concepts for sequencing events and will help your child understand beginning, middle, and end of a story. Prediction is a valuable comprehension skill. Cultivate it early.

- Your child will soon be ready for books with unfamiliar characters who interact with each other in events that may be unfamiliar. Reread stories with more complicated plots several times, explaining the characters and setting.

- Try to make connections between the story you are reading and your child's experiences. Take mini field trips to see things you have read about.

- Gradually read more books that introduce children from different cultural and ethnic backgrounds.

Soon your child will be begging for her favorites and you'll have yours as well.

Three

The First Years
Birth to Age 3

* * *

Have you ever rightly considered what the mere ability to read means? That it is the key which admits us to the whole world of thought and fancy and imagination? To the company of saint and sage, of the wisest and wittiest at their wisest and wittiest moment? That it enables us to see with the keenest of eyes, hear with the finest ears, and listen to the sweetest voice of all times?

James Russell Lowell

I was a first-time mother. My newborn daughter and I had been home from the hospital only three days. I was more than a little nervous. Far away from close family members, I was delighted when an experienced mom dropped by for a visit. I welcomed the opportunity to talk to a veteran. She brought a gift with her as well as some sage advice for a new parent. "I always give books as baby gifts," she said, handing me a colorfully wrapped package. "I hope you'll start reading aloud to Emily right away. I've read aloud to all my children." As a school librarian I was already a believer in reading aloud, but to have a seasoned mother confirm the importance of this practice with a personal visit and testimony strengthened my resolve to get started early.

That evening as I rocked my fretful baby asleep, I began reading from the book my visitor had brought. It contained poems and nursery rhymes set off with Tasha Tudor illustrations. That book is still on our shelf while other gifts have long been forgotten. Whenever I read the inscription on the flyleaf I think of those early months and the security and comfort reading aloud brought to my newborn and me. I'm especially grateful to that dedicated mother for her example and the interest she showed in me.

The first three years are special ones for you and your child. They are also among the most important in terms of forming lifelong patterns and learnings. Your baby can comprehend and learn far beyond what you might imagine. Take advantage of every opportunity to read aloud!

In the first half of this chapter you'll meet several children ranging in age from six months to two-and-a-half years old. Their characteristics and descriptions are composites of many children I've known, including my own children. Perhaps you'll recognize your own child among the group. There are hundreds of books on the market for children in this age group. We'll recommend the best in the second half of the chapter.

The Children

Alex is six months old. His parents have two older children and know that their days of having Alex stay where they put him are nearly over. He is just beginning to satisfy his desire to move about. Only last week, while his mother was in the kitchen, he rolled across the family room and pulled over a potted plant.

When he sits in his high chair, a favorite game is dropping toys to the floor. His older brothers laugh and clap at his antics but quickly tire of picking up the rattles. Alex seems to be talking to them as he plays the game and is a very sociable companion. Alex's mother knows that even though he won't begin talking for several months, he already understands a great deal.

She encourages his older brothers to talk with him whenever they are around and not with the baby talk they seemed to think was appropriate when he was born. Although Alex can't respond in comprehensible words to the conversation around him, his big brown eyes look to each of his brothers as they talk about their school day.

Another favorite game of this six month old is hide and seek. His brothers put a blanket in front of their faces and quickly pull it aside, gleefully calling out, "Peek-a-boo!" The best time for reading stories to Alex is just before his nap or bedtime. He isn't the greatest of cuddlers, but after a bath and nursing, his mother always reads from a favorite rhyme book.

Karen just celebrated her first birthday. She began walking at nine months and her insatiable curiosity has already forced her family to completely rearrange the house. She is an incredible climber and only last week stopped her mother's heart when she climbed from the kitchen chair to the top of the counter. She was on her way to the top of the refrigerator when Mom interrupted her ascent.

Although she is an extraordinarily active child, Karen can frequently be observed sitting motionless while gazing at an object or person. Sometimes she stares out the window, sometimes at her mother, and often at a favorite toy, absorbed in learning details about the world around her.

When her father arrives home from work and calls her name, Karen runs to greet him. If she's in a cooperative mood, she'll throw him a kiss. Karen is interested in everything—controls on the stove, water in the toilet bowl, even dust under the bed. She leads her mother on a merry chase from one exciting exploration to another. Her mother wisely doesn't confine her to a playpen but child-proofs the house wherever possible.

Karen's mother knows how important reading is and since Karen is fascinated with animals of any kind, they spend time every day reading aloud animal picture books. Mom says the names of the animals and points Karen's finger to the appropriate words and pictures. They make animal sounds and have a good time together. Mom can usually tell when Karen's attention is beginning to wane and puts the books away. They will read again at bedtime, even if only for a short time.

If he weren't packaged in such a small body, an observer would certify that eighteen-month-old Jason was a bona fide adolescent. He is definitely asserting his independence and mixes that characteristic with a fair amount of negativism.

He no longer worships his older sister, Sarah, and frequently appears to relish interfering with her model building. At times Jason's only redeeming quality is his ability to engage in delightful conversations. His appealing manner, when he chooses to exhibit it, entrances his grandparents.

Jason loves outdoor activity and a part of every day is a trip to the local park. He swings, balances on the animal toys, examines the grass, and plays in the sandbox. His mother tries to interest him in watching *Sesame Street* but finds that more than ten minutes of sitting still is too much for Jason.

She has discovered, however, that reading books with pictures of trucks or fire engines will keep Jason interested for up to twenty minutes. He never tires of naming the vehicles and naturally, Jason and Mom make sound effects to accompany the pictures.

Maria is a nonstop talker. At two and a half she most of all wants to know "why." She spends long periods of time building block towers. She enjoys watching *Sesame Street* or *Mister Rogers* while working with her toys. Drawing and pretending to write on paper with crayons are favorite activities also.

Her ability to sit still and concentrate for extended periods makes reading aloud to her a pleasure. She frequently brings favorites to her mother with a request to read. Maria shops at garage sales with her mother and always gets to pick out one or two bargains of her own from the book table.

Maria's most often requested excursion involves a trip to the petting zoo. She would go there every day if she could. Her mom capitalizes on this interest by reading every kind of animal story she can find.

Although Maria is curious, she resists all of her mother's efforts to teach her. She is much happier when exploring, questioning, and learning on her own. She loves routine and becomes very upset if bedtime is not accompanied by at least three stories. She has her own special way of counting the stories and becomes very annoyed if her mother disagrees with her accounting. After a busy day, her mother is grateful that after three, Maria will settle down to turn the pages on her own and gradually fall off to sleep surrounded by her books. Her mother tiptoes in later to remove the books from Maria's bed.

The Choices

As parents we will make many choices for our children as they grow. The choices we make for them in their younger years will begin to shape the interests and values that determine the choices they will make for themselves as they mature. The more exposure your children have to good books, the more frequently they will choose the best for themselves. Therefore you need to have a rationale and guide for the choices you make. The books you read to your children should be age-appropriate and well written and illustrated. All of the books I have chosen to include in the chapters ahead meet those criteria. You will also want to choose books that espouse the beliefs and values that you hold.

The read aloud selections for children ages birth to three are grouped in nine categories: Bible story and prayer books, participation books, wordless books, alphabet books, concept books, Mother Goose and nursery rhymes, poetry, picture books, and counting books. Age categories are somewhat arbitrary, so you will find that many of the recommendations in this chapter are also appropriate for older children. The choices are arranged by author; once you discover one you like, check out more of his or her titles. Each of the recommended titles in the following chapters was in print and available online from http://www.amazon.com or could be ordered at your local bookstore when this book went to press. However, book buyers are fickle, and sometimes even old favorites go out of print almost overnight. Amazon.com will help you search for out-of-print books, however, and your public library will almost always have older books available for checkout. Also consult resource D, which contains a list of book-related Web sites.

Bible Story and Prayer Books

The Bible Story and Prayer Books category is included for each age level, since as children mature, their needs change. The recommendations here are suitable for that very first Bible story read-aloud.

Anglund, Joan Walsh. *Prayer Is a Gentle Way of Being with God.* Harold Shaw, 1999.

Anglund's simple words and charming illustrations talk about prayer in ways a child will understand. The message speaks to adults as well.

Hague, Michael. *A Child's Book of Prayers.* Henry Holt, 1998.

The traditional childhood prayers are reverently illustrated with five colors, gold borders, and easy-to-read type.

Lindvall, Ella K. *Read Aloud Bible Stories,* vols. 1–4. Moody, 1982, 1985, 1990, and 1995.

Lindvall understands the young child's needs for simplicity. These stories have been written with the interest and attention span of the two to three year old in mind, and the illustrations do an excellent job of enhancing the stories.

Rock, Lois. *All Year Long.* Illustrated by Louise Rawlings. Lion, 1997.

Prayers to celebrate the changing seasons and God's care for his creatures. Other titles in the series include *Safe This Night; Bright Star Night;* and *Sad News, Glad News.*

Sattgast, L. J. *The Rhyme Bible.* Illustrated by Toni Goffe. Gold 'n' Honey, 1996.

With simple but well-done rhymes and winsome illustrations, this toddler Bible is sure to be a favorite at your house.

Participation Books

Participation books are appropriate for your child's first read aloud experience. The books, usually made of cloth or heavy cardboard so that tiny fingers cannot tear the pages, are compact and have simple words and pictures. Although some titles may be found in your public library, you will want to purchase several titles for your child.

Anderson, Deb. *I Can! God Helps Me from A to Z.* Chariot Victor, 1995.

An ABC board book for tiny hands to hold. The illustrations bring the alphabet to life and the text focuses on things a child can do with God's help.

Henderson, Felicity. *Wake Up, Everybody.* Lion, 1995.

> Daily events that happen at everyone's house are celebrated in this attractively illustrated board book. Other board books by Henderson include *Baby's Day* and *Hello Baby.*

Wildsmith, Brian. *Brian Wildsmith's ABC.* Star Bright, 1996.

> The vivid colors and shapes of Wildsmith's illustrations will attract your baby and the sturdy cardboard covers will withstand even the most energetic reader.

Wordless Books

Wordless books allow the child's imagination to create a story of his own. The illustrations become the focal point and the story can have a variety of interpretations depending on your mood.

Hutchins, Pat. *Changes, Changes.* Aladdin Paperbacks, 1987.

> Does your child play with colorful wooden blocks? If so, he'll enjoy this clever wordless book. A pair of wooden dolls rearrange blocks on each page as they build their home, put out a fire with their block fire engine, and eventually sail away in their block boat.

Spier, Peter. *Noah's Ark.* Picture Yearling, 1992.

> The biblical story of Noah and the ark is meticulously illustrated by Peter Spier. Although Spier's translation of a Dutch poem "The Flood" appears in its entirety at the beginning, you're on your own with wordless pictures for the remainder of the book. Examine the drawings carefully to see Noah cope with a hive of bees and a recalcitrant donkey. My favorite illustration shows the inside of the ark after Noah and his menagerie have exited. Quite a mess! This Caldecott Medal winner will be a winner on your bookshelf.

Tafuri, Nancy. *Have You Seen My Duckling?* Beech Tree, 1996.

This book is wordless, except for the phrase "Have you seen my duckling?" which is repeated from time to time throughout the story. You and your child will enjoy looking for the lost duckling, who is off adventuring, oblivious to the fact that he is missed.

Alphabet Books

Alphabet books are primarily designed to teach the alphabet, something every child needs to know in order to learn to read. But they serve other purposes as well. You and your child will learn to appreciate a variety of different artists as you compare the ways they have chosen to present the alphabet. While learning the alphabet, your child will increase his vocabulary and enhance his language development. Alphabet books comprise a fascinating part of children's literature, and many different illustrators have put their unique stamp on the letters that comprise our English language.

Boynton, Sandra. *A-to-Z.* Little Simon, 1995.

Your baby-toddler will love this alphabet board book. Boynton doesn't take her alphabet too seriously and silliness is the order of the day. Chuckle, giggle, and then laugh right out loud as you read this one together.

Hague, Kathleen. *Alphabears.* Illustrated by Michael Hague. Live Oak Media, 1985.

Imagine twenty-six different teddy bears, each with a unique personality. There are male and female bears, and each one is featured in a full-page painting with a charming rhyme. These are the most lovable bears I've ever seen.

Suess, Dr. *Dr. Seuss's ABC.* Random House, 1996.

This timeless favorite is now available in a board book format along with three other titles: *The Foot Book: Dr.*

Seuss's Wacky Book of Opposites; Mr. Brown Can Moo, Can You?: Dr. Seuss's Book of Wonderful Noises; and *There's a Wocket in My Pocket: Dr. Seuss's Book of Ridiculous Rhymes.* These were all favorites at our house in the early 70s and your child will love them too.

Concept Books

Reading aloud from this category of books will give you countless opportunities to teach your child while also having fun. A concept is defined as an "abstract notion." Through these entertaining read-alouds your child will begin to understand how the world works.

Crews, Donald. *Freight Train.* Beech Tree, 1996.

Is your child fascinated by a passing train? If so, he'll love to turn the pages in *Freight Train.* The pictures and print are clean and sized for the preschooler. He'll learn about colors, varieties of train cars, and the concepts by, through, and over. The train seems to be moving as you turn the pages. Other Crews books for the child interested in vehicles are *School Bus* and *Truck.*

Hoban, Tana. *Of Colors and Things.* Greenwillow, 1989.

Full-color photographs of real objects offer visual delight and will help your child learn colors very quickly. Other outstanding concept books by Hoban include *Look Up, Look Down; Is It Larger? Is It Smaller?; Spiral, Curve, Fan-shapes and Lines; Dig, Drill, Dump, Fill; Shapes and Things; Circles, Triangles, and Squares; Over, Under, and Through; Round and Round and Round;* and *Push-Pull, Empty-Full.*

Kalan, Robert. *Blue Sea.* Illustrated by Donald Crews. Greenwillow, 1987.

The concepts of big and little are clearly presented, and before long you'll find your toddler "reading" along with you. The repetition of phrases gives a poetic feel to the text, and the deep blue pages with brightly colored letters and fish put the reader right into the ocean.

Pienkowski, Jan. *Time.* Little Simon, 1991.

If your toddler likes clocks, pick up this board book that contains clocks showing different times and events throughout the day and night.

Rockwell, Anne. *Planes.* Puffin, 1993.

Are planes, trucks, boats, or cars big at your house? Anne Rockwell has written the perfect books to satisfy even the most curious transportation buff. Bright watercolors and large type will make this and other Rockwell titles favorites of all children: *Trucks, Boats,* and *Cars.*

Scarry, Richard. *Best Word Book Ever.* Golden, 1980.

Tiny drawings, meticulous labels, and very busy pages are Richard Scarry's trademarks. This book provides a painless way to introduce hundreds of new words and concepts to your toddler. Every home should have one or more of Scarry's books. Other titles include *What Do People Do All Day? Cars and Trucks and Things That Go,* and *Early Words.*

Mother Goose and Nursery Rhymes

You probably won't need more than one or two Mother Goose treasuries unless you're a serious collector. So take your time and browse through several before you make a final selection.

Hague, Michael. *Mother Goose: A Collection of Classic Nursery Rhymes.* Henry Holt, 1988.

This collection of classic nursery rhymes is beautifully illustrated in a soft, old-fashioned style. Since there is only one rhyme and illustration per page, the volume is especially appropriate for the younger child. An index of first lines is helpful.

Opie, Iona Archibald. *My Very First Mother Goose.* Illustrated by Rosemary Wells. Candlewick, 1996.

> I absolutely adore this collection. Opie has chosen all of my favorite rhymes and I'm crazy about Wells's sense of humor that shines through her irrepressible illustrations. When my children have their first children, this will be the collection I give.

Yolen, Jane. *Jane Yolen's Mother Goose Songbook.* Illustrated by Rosekrans Hoffman. Boyds Mills, 1992.

> If you enjoy music, you'll want to acquire this song-book. Musical arrangements for piano and guitar are provided for more than forty-five Mother Goose songs.

Poetry

Poems are word pictures, written to capture the feeling or mood of a certain time or place. Or they can be quirky, humorous rhymes to tickle your funny bone. When a new snow has just fallen, read A. A. Milne's "The More It Snows." As you drive over the highway to Grandmother's house for Thanksgiving Day, the lines "Over the river and through the woods, to Grandmother's house we go" just beg to be recited. One or two poetry collections belong in every family's library. Poetry has always captivated the young child. Rhythm and rhyme invite clapping and bouncing. With the newest reading research showing the importance of phonemic awareness to a child's reading success, poetry is more than just nice, it's absolutely necessary! Spend time having fun with rhyme and rhythm every single day!

Brown, Marc Tolon. *Play Rhymes.* Puffin, 1993.

Teach your child these twelve toe-tapping rhymes. Illustrations for hand motions are included as well as music for six of the rhymes. Look for finger rhymes such as "The Eensy, Weensy Spider" and "Where Is Thumbkin?" and hand rhymes with illustrations of fourteen hand games.

Cole, Joanna, and Stephanie Calmenson. *Pat-a-Cake and Other Play Rhymes.* Illustrated by Alan Tiegreen. Morrow Junior, 1992.

I love the organization of this charming book: finger and hand rhymes, toe and foot rhymes, face rhymes, tickling rhymes, knee and foot riding rhymes, and dancing rhymes. You'll find hours of fun here.

Dyer, Jane. *Animal Crackers: A Delectable Collection of Pictures, Poems and Lullabies for the Very Young.* Little, Brown, 1996.

Once you check this book out of the library, you'll want to purchase your own copy. *Delectable* is definitely the operative word, not only for the fabulous collection of poems, nursery rhymes, and lullabies, but for the scrumptious illustrations. One of my childhood favorites recited whenever my mother put water on to boil, "Polly, Put the Kettle On," is included as well as Eugene Field's Dutch lullaby "Wynken, Blynken, and Nod."

Frank, Josette. *Poems to Read to the Very Young.* Illustrated by Eloise Wilkins. Random House Childrens, 1988.

This should be the first poetry collection you buy. With only thirty-two pages, both book and baby will fit nicely on your lap. The expressive illustrations by Eloise Wilkins bring to life the poetry of such favorites as A. A. Milne, Christina Rosetti, and Robert Louis Stevenson.

Hague, Michael. *Sleep, Baby, Sleep: Lullabies and Night Poems.* William Morrow, 1994.

Marvelous lullabies and favorite poems that feature the night are beautifully illustrated by Michael Hague. Also

included are more than two dozen musical arrange-
ments for piano and guitar.

Prelutsky, Jack. *The Random House Book of Poetry for Children.* Illustrated by Arnold Lobel. Random House, 1983.

This substantial anthology of over five hundred of the best-loved poems for children creatively groups poetry into thematic sections. Editor Jack Prelutsky, an out-standing poet in his own right, has written a special introductory poem for each section. Arnold Lobel, well-known for his *Frog and Toad* series, has contributed hundreds of detailed drawings and paintings.

Prelutsky, Jack. *Read Aloud Rhymes for the Very Young.* Illustrated by Marc Tolon Brown. A. A. Knopf, 1986.

"Can't I just finish the story I'm reading here in my book?" says the character in the Eleanor Farjeon poem "Bedtime," one of dozens of old and new poems in this volume. Jack Prelutsky has an ear for the very best and Marc Brown interprets the poems in fresh ways.

Picture Books

The simple stories contained in this list can be read over and over. They will be enjoyed (by your child, if not you) as much on their tenth or twentieth reading as on the first. That is the true test of a read aloud picture book, after all—does your child want to hear it every night? If your child of two or three is ready for more complex plots, look ahead to chapter 4, where dozens of longer picture books are featured. And of course, you have permission to read any of your favorites from chapter 3 well after your child turns three.

Baby Bear's Treasury. Candlewick, 1995.

This is a fabulous collection of the best children's authors and illustrators doing their stuff for the very young set. The list of contributors reads like a Who's Who; you and your child will enjoy every one of the twenty-five stories for the very, very young.

Barton, Byron. *The Little Red Hen.* HarperCollins Juvenile, 1997.

This retelling of the well-known story of the red hen is perfect for the youngest child. Vivid but simple illustrations emphasize basic colors and shapes while the text is predictable and readily memorized. You'll want to have this one in your permanent collection.

Box, Su. *You Are Very Special.* Illustrated by Susie Poole. Lion, 1996.

This book is made special by the surprise that will show your child just how special he is. The illustrations are engaging and the message is one you'll want your child to hear often while he's growing up.

Bridwell, Norman. *Clifford the Big Red Dog.* Scholastic Trade, 1988.

Everybody loves Clifford, in spite of his character flaws and unpleasant habits, such as chewing shoes. He provides the companionship, comfort, and protection that children adore in their pets, and his mistress Emily Elizabeth wouldn't be without him.

Brown, Margaret Wise. *Goodnight Moon.* Illustrated by Clement Hurd. Harper-Collins Childrens, 1991.

A perfect story for bedtime read-aloud. The rhyming words and restful illustrations will help you move your child (who will relate to the fictional bunny's reluctance to go to bed) from busy activities to a peaceful bedtime. Held in high esteem by parents everywhere, this classic is a must for your bookshelf.

Another often overlooked Brown book is *Wait Til the Moon Is Full,* the story of a little raccoon's eagerness to see the full moon. Still other favorites by Brown include *The Little Fireman, Little Fur Family,* and *The Runaway Bunny.*

Eastman, P. D. *Are You My Mother?* Random House Childrens, 1988.

Although this title is an easy reader, the story line is one that will entrance your toddler. A baby bird falls out of the nest and tries to find his mother. Before he finds his way back to the nest, he asks the question, "Are you my mother?" of a kitten, hen, cow, and even a steam shovel. Your young one will delight in figuring out who the bird's real mother is long before the baby bird does.

Flack, Marjorie. *Ask Mr. Bear.* Aladdin Paperbacks, 1986.

Chances are you remember this book from your own childhood. Danny needs a birthday present for his mother. After consulting Mrs. Hen, Mrs. Goose, and numerous other barnyard animals, Danny finally goes to Mr. Bear, who comes up with a surprising idea—a bear hug. You'll have plenty of opportunity to do your own animal impressions when you read this perennial favorite, and it's always fun to finish off the story with your own bear hugs. You'll also want to read *The Story about Ping,* the tale of a little duck alone on the Yangtze River. It is a beautiful reminder of the importance of home and family.

Ginsburg, Mirra. *The Chick and the Duckling.* Illustrated by Jose and Ariane Aruego. Aladdin Paperbacks, 1988.

Bold, colorful drawings illustrate the simple text of this Russian tale. Chick and Duckling hatch into the world at the same time. They play "anything you can do, I can do also," until Chick discovers that Duckling can swim. The predictable results illustrate the importance of realizing our unique talents. Another excellent folktale by Ginsburg is *The Strongest One of All.*

Hill, Eric. *Where's Spot?* Putnam, 1980.

If you don't have *Where's Spot?* on your bookshelf, you're missing more than just a puppy. Opportunities for learning and language development abound in this story of a mother dog searching for her missing offspring, Spot. The search for Spot is made even more interesting by a lift-the-flap feature. Your toddler will want to hear this one (as well as lift the flaps) over and over and over. Other Spot titles include *Spot's First Words, Spot Looks at Colors,* and *Spot Looks at Shapes.*

Hutchins, Pat. *Rosie's Walk.* Aladdin Paperbacks, 1983.

Rosie the hen goes for a walk never realizing that a fox is close behind her. Your preschooler will howl with glee as the fox runs into several misadventures while Rosie, oblivious to what's happening behind her, gets back in time for dinner, unharmed. Hutchins has a knack for writing and illustrations that entrance the very young child (and his parents).

Johnson, Crockett. *Harold and the Purple Crayon.* HarperCollins, 1981.

Toddlers will be mesmerized as Harold creates pictures with his purple crayon. They will want to hear this time-less favorite over and over as they try to figure out just how Harold is able to do whatever he wants with only his imagination and a purple crayon. Just make sure you keep crayons of all colors under lock and key after you've read this one. Other titles in the series are *Harold's Trip to the Sky, Harold's ABC, Harold's Fairy Tale: Further Adventures with the Purple Crayon,* and *Harold's Circus.*

Krauss, Ruth. *The Carrot Seed.* Illustrated by Crockett Johnson. HarperCollins, 1988.

This is the perfect story to read aloud when you and your child plant that first seed together. The little boy in this simple story has faith that his seed will come up even though his family is certain it won't. Many adults still prize their own yellowed copies of *The Carrot Seed,* first published in 1967, and dig it out whenever they need an encouraging word. Another highly recom-mended title by Krauss is *A Hole Is to Dig: A First Book of First Definitions.*

Leimert, Karen Mezek. *Good Night Blessings.* Thomas Nelson, 1994.

> A simple goodnight prayer thanking God for all the
> blessings of nature. The illustrations are serene and
> there's an added bonus—each of the featured topics
> (such as rain, sky, fish) is highlighted in large black type
> at the top of each two-page spread. Your child's associa-
> tion of your spoken words with their printed counter-
> parts will occur naturally as you reread the story, partic-
> ularly if you point to the word as you read it, moving
> your finger along the letters as you blend them together.

Lucado, Max. *Just in Case You Ever Wonder.* Illustrated by Toni Goffe. Wordkids,
1992.

> A wonderful affirmation of love, both a parent's and
> God's, for a child. Lucado's promises to his own three
> daughters inspired this book.

Martin, Bill Jr. *Brown Bear, Brown Bear, What Do You See?* Illustrated by Eric
Carle. Holt, Rinehart and Winston, 1983.

> This title combines all of the elements a successful tod-
> dler book needs—bright illustrations, simple, predictable
> text, and an elegant concept. Before long you will find
> that your toddler has memorized the words and is "read-
> ing" with you. Brown bear, red bird, yellow duck, and
> blue horse will soon become bedtime favorites at your
> house. See resource E for a list of additional "pre-
> dictable" books, those titles that have repetitive lan-
> guage patterns and repeated or cumulative story events.
> Predictable books encourage memorizing and help a
> child learn how to sequence a chain of events.

Potter, Beatrix. *The Tale of Peter Rabbit.* Frederick Warne, 1987.

> Peter Rabbit is part of the cultural literacy of growing up.
> Getting your child acquainted with Flopsy, Mopsy, and
> Peter Cottontail and vicariously experiencing the conse-
> quences of trespassing in Mr. McGregor's garden should
> be part of every child's read aloud life.

Trent, John. *There's a Duck in My Closet!* Illustrated by Judy Love. Tommy Nelson, 1993.

> This bedtime read-aloud is the perfect antidote to those fears of the dark. The exquisite illustrations are a perfect accompaniment to the story in rhyme. Psychologist John Trent knows how to calm nighttime jitters with humor and a positive approach.

Wallace, John. *Little Bean's Friend.* Harper Festival, 1996.

> Little Bean is an engaging tyke to whom your toddler will readily relate. In this book she makes a new friend, a very exciting adventure for every small child. Toddlers (and moms) will identify with Bean's busy day.

Wells, Rosemary. *Bunny Cakes.* Dial Books for Young Readers, 1997.

> Max and Ruby, Wells's two endearing bunnies, are up to nonsense again in this the latest of thirteen titles in the series. The big decision is whether to make Grandma an angel surprise cake with raspberry-fluff icing, Ruby's choice, or to go with Max's favorite, red-hot marshmallow squirters. Other titles include *Bunny Money, Max's Dragon Shirt,* and *Max's First Word.*

Wells, Rosemary. *Forest of Dreams.* Illustrated by Susan Jeffers. Voyager Picture Book, 1996.

> This title by Wells is so different from what she usually does I've chosen to list it separately. The simple text and joyous pictures are a celebration of the wonders of God's creation in nature. You will feel as though you're actually outdoors as spring bursts forth in Jeffers's stunning illustrations.

Counting Books

Children are captivated by counting. This selection of counting books will give you and your child an amazing assortment of things to count, and the early introduction to numbers will make math seem easy when school begins.

Bang, Molly. *Ten, Nine, Eight.* Greenwillow, 1983.

A simple backwards counting book based on a little girl's goodnight lullaby. After you finish counting the toes, stuffed animals, and empty shoes in the colorful pictures, you'll want to do the same in your child's room.

Carle, Eric. *1, 2, 3 to the Zoo: A Counting Book.* Putnam, 1987.

Animals are a surefire subject for a counting book, and in Eric Carle's version they are part of a train going to the zoo. If a trip to the zoo is on your agenda, be sure to read this book before, during, and after.

Cooner, Donna D. *Count Your Blessings.* Illustrated by Kim Simons. Tommy Nelson, 1995.

Based on the familiar hymn "Count Your Many Blessings," this colorful counting book enumerates the many things for which you and your child should give thanks. Another excellent title by Cooner is *The World God Made.*

Crews, Donald. *Ten Black Dots.* Mulberry, 1995.

What can you do with ten black dots? Donald Crews, in his inimitable graphic style, shows you. One dot can make a sun, three dots a snowman's face, and eight dots the wheels on a train.

Hague, Kathleen. *Numbears: A Counting Book.* Illustrated by Michael Hague. Henry Holt, 1986.

If teddy bears are in vogue at your house, you'll love this counting-rhyme book featuring twelve lovable bears, each with something for you and your child to count.

Hoban, Tana. *Count and See.* Simon and Schuster, 1972.

This prize-winning photographer has put together a counting book that emphasizes real objects with which children can identify. The photos are black and white and accompanied by white dots on black pages so that children can practice their counting in several ways.

Hutchins, Pat. *1 Hunter.* William Morrow, 1982.

A lone hunter sets out for the jungle and along the way he encounters 2 elephants, 3 giraffes, 7 crocodiles, and a variety of other jungle creatures. A creative contribution to your counting book collection.

Schlein, Miriam. *More Than One.* Illustrated by Donald Crews. Greenwillow, 1996.

This unusual counting book will disabuse you of the notion that one is simply one. How about one pair of shoes? Two. One baseball team? Nine. Well, you get the idea and so will your child.

Four

Off to School
Ages 4 to 7

• • •

There is no Frigate like a Book
To take us Lands away
Nor any Coursers like a Page
Of prancing Poetry—

This Traverse may the poorest take
Without oppress of Toll—
How frugal is the Chariot
That bears the Human Soul.

Emily Dickinson

S ending your children off to school is a scary experience. I remember when mine started preschool and
kindergarten. One morning they weren't all mine anymore. I no longer controlled how they spent every
waking minute or what they learned. Suddenly the time we'd
spent together in those first three years seemed over-

whelmingly important. But it was over! Now I just had to trust and pray that while away from home, they would value and remember the lessons we'd learned together. I spent all of two or three days contemplating this dreadful separation. Then I went out for breakfast and prepared to enjoy the flip side of the coin.

My children made new friends, learned new skills, and gained confidence and independence. Books were a wonderful source of connection to our family in these beginning school years. Reading aloud together gave us reasons to sit down and talk about school, friends, problems, and the meaning of life. They gave us a way to spend time together and keep in touch.

In the first part of this chapter you will meet several children who are in the beginning years of their school careers. Their attitudes about formal reading instruction are beginning to form and they are soaking up new skills and information every day. Perhaps you'll recognize your own child among the group. In the second part of the chapter you'll find books that are especially recommended for reading aloud to children ages four through seven.

The Children

Jeremy is four years old. His father appreciates his exuberant and bold nature, but Jeremy's mom is constantly reminding Jeremy that he's only four years old and can't ride his bicycle down the front steps. Jeremy is a study in contrasts. He often walks down the street to play with a close friend, carefully remaining on the sidewalk per his mother's instructions. However, in an instant he can turn into a verbal whirlwind and tell his mother he hates her.

Vigorous physical activities are part of the church preschool program that Jeremy attends. He builds enthusiastically with big blocks and plays vivid imaginary games with his closest friend, John. He loves the Bible stories his teacher reads, especially the ones that involve action.

A boisterous sense of humor gives Jeremy a special appreciation for stories with outrageous plots. He loves detailed drawings and is able to name all of the pictures in his alphabet and word books. Jeremy is beginning to develop a strong sense of the difference between being good and bad. He knows that God wants him to be good and prays with his mom or dad each night. His prayers are expansive, asking God to bless his friends, grandparents, and even his pet frog.

Adam has just begun kindergarten. At five years old he loves everyone, especially his mother and his kindergarten teacher. He spends a great deal of time talking and tells his mother all about what goes on each morning at school. They are cutting, pasting, playing, singing, stringing, dancing, running, and jumping. He wants to duplicate all of his school activities at home.

Although he has always loved having stories read aloud to him, now that he's five he can't get enough reading aloud. Adam's mom shares this happy task with her older children. Adam has many close friends, but mom wisely invites only one at a time to play. Sharing friends is still a difficult assignment for this five year old.

When he misbehaves, Adam responds well to time-out in his bedroom. Five minutes away from the family usually results in a contrite, cooperative child.

Although Adam falls asleep quickly after bedtime stories, he frequently wakes up with nightmares. His parents are careful to read quiet, friendly stories before bedtime. They always end their bedtime story hour with a prayer from Adam's favorite book of prayers, asking God to watch over Adam while he is sleeping. Adam asks many questions about God and believes that he is responsible for everything. The death of Adam's grandfather generated many questions, and his parents were grateful to have a book like *What Happens*

When We Die? to read aloud to him. For a complete list of kindergarten accomplishments in reading, see resource F.

When she was five, Elizabeth was a delight. Now six, she's a real crybaby. School is hard, her friends don't like her, and her feelings are always bruised. Loving Elizabeth takes lots of patience. Surprisingly her teacher sees none of this negative behavior, although Elizabeth does have a difficult time sitting still and remaining quiet for an entire morning.

But her mood can change quickly. When she can forget about the emotional ups and downs of being six, her relationship with the world and life is enthusiastic. She loves to read, write, and draw. She talks nonstop and has strong opinions about her likes and dislikes. She is very curious about babies and how they've come to be. She wants to know about death and where people go after they die.

She is an enthusiastic participant in church and Sunday school. She loves to sing and has memorized many songs with their accompanying motions. Elizabeth is learning to read in school. She brings home simple books and carefully sounds out each word. She would like to play school with her younger brother, but his attention span is too short for Elizabeth.

Her mother sometimes feels that a small tornado has passed through the kitchen when Elizabeth arrives on the scene. Once she's had a snack and shared the woes of her day, Elizabeth's bright and sunny nature returns. Going to school all day is definitely hard work. For a complete list of first-grade reading accomplishments, see resource F.

Seth is seven years old. A new baby has just arrived and Seth is a big help to his mother. He empties the garbage, makes his own bed, and cleans up his room. His mother was concerned about how Seth would respond to a sibling, but he has assumed the big brother role with ease.

Seth is an excellent reader and enjoys books about real boys his own age who do exciting things. Animals, space travel, and strange bugs also intrigue him. During weekly trips to the library, he checks out several books he can read by himself.

Seth is preoccupied with the idea of heaven, probably because of his interest in space. He wants to know where it is, how God gets there, and how it is possible that God can see everything and be everywhere while remaining in heaven.

Perhaps Seth's most disagreeable trait is his obsession with perfection. He dislikes mistakes in himself as well as in his family and friends. He doesn't take correction well and often tries to cover up his errors. He frequently dawdles while dressing himself, and his mom sets a timer to keep him focused on the task.

With the arrival of a new baby, there has been less time for reading aloud, but Seth's teacher has a contest going at school, so Seth is motivated and reminds his mom or dad daily that he needs to read with them. For a complete list of second-grade reading accomplishments, see resource F.

The Choices

The choices from which to make your read aloud selections for children between the ages of four and seven will be grouped into the following categories: Bible story and scriptural application books; picture books; books for the independent reader; concept, counting, and alphabet books for the older child; folk and fairy tales; and poetry. Each of the recommended titles was in print and available online from http://www.amazon.com or from your local bookstore when this book went to press. Also consult resource D, which contains a list of book-related Web sites.

Bible Story and Scriptural Application Books

Bible story and scriptural application books will be especially helpful as you guide your children spiritually and attempt to answer the many questions and concerns they have about God.

Carlson, Melody. *Gold and Honey Bible.* Illustrated by Dennis Ochsner. Gold 'n' Honey, 1997.

> Well-done contemporary illustrations, fresh language, and Bible story retellings that flow make this version a must to have.

Egermeier, Elsie. *Egermeier's Bible Story Book.* Revised by Arlene S. Hall. Warner, 1969.

> When choosing a Bible story book, two important considerations are quality of writing and adherence to biblical truth. The updated version of this classic (first printed in 1922) has both. Excellent illustrations and brief but well-written stories that children will enjoy make this mandatory for your family bookshelf. The index of stories is especially helpful. Other titles by Egermeier include *Egermeier's Favorite Bible Stories* (thirty stories adapted for younger readers), *Egermeier's Picture-Story Life of Jesus* (stories of the life of Christ adapted from the big story book), and *Picture Story Bible ABC Book.*

Henley, Karyn. *God's Story: The Bible Told as One Story.* Tyndale, 1998.

> A verse-by-verse retelling of Scripture with over eight hundred age-appropriate stories. The reading level is approximately second grade, so you can transition from using this book as a read aloud Bible to encouraging your child to read it on her own. This book will serve very nicely as a bridge between Bible story books and full-text Bibles.

Hill, Dave. *The Boy Who Gave His Lunch Away.* Illustrated by Betty Wind. Concordia, 1993.

> This series of Arch paperback Bible stories in rhyme has withstood the test of time. Children adore them; they're compact, fast paced, and colorfully illustrated. First published in the '60s, there are now over one hundred titles in the series by different authors and illustrators. Our family favorites included *The Boy with a Sling, The Braggy King of Babylon,* and *The Lame Man Who Walked Again.* Some of the individual stories have been collected in two hardcover collections: *Children of the Old Testament* and *Children of the New Testament.*

Nystrom, Carolyn. *Who Is Jesus?* Illustrated by Wayne A. Hanna. Moody, 1993.

> This title, one of several in *The Children's Bible Basics* series, is a simple introduction to the life and mission of Jesus. All of the titles in the series explain Christian concepts and principles in a way that children can understand. The text is based on scriptural references, and the colorful illustrations and meaningful applications to a child's own life are outstanding. When your children stump you with theological questions, reach for one of these titles: *What Is Prayer? Why Do I Do Things Wrong? What Is a Christian? The Holy Spirit in Me, What Is the Bible? What Is the Church? Growing Jesus' Way, What Happens When We Die?* and *Jesus Is No Secret.*

Tangvald, Christine Harder, and Julie Smith. *A Child's Book of Prayers.* Illustrated by Frances and Richard Hook. Chariot Victor, 1993.

> This collection of simple children's prayers is beautifully illustrated. The prayers are well written and the illustrations are warm and reverent.

Picture Books

Picture books tell a simple story and are accompanied by colorful illustrations. The true test of a good picture book is its enduring readability. You'll soon learn which authors in this category have a knack for catching the interest and attention of both you and your children. Then you can find other titles by that same author. I've selected authors and titles that survived the read aloud test either in our home or in the various classrooms and libraries in which I've worked. However, don't consider just my opinion when you begin choosing books for your children. Consult resource C for books that contain the recommendations of other authors from a variety of perspectives.

Bemelmans, Ludwig. *Madeline's Rescue.* Viking, 1951.

Madeline and her eleven friends attend a boarding school in Paris. These charming tales are told in rhymes that children love and will quickly be memorized. Other titles include *Madeline, Madeline and the Bad Hat, Madeline and the Gypsies,* and *Madeline's Christmas.*

Bennett, William J., editor. *The Children's Book of Virtues.* Illustrated by Michael Hague. Simon and Schuster, 1995.

This children's counterpart to Bennett's best-selling *The Book of Virtues* for adults contains read aloud selections from classics that emphasize courage, perseverance, responsibility, work, self-discipline, compassion, faith, honesty, loyalty, and friendship. My favorite is a tale that was often told when I was growing up as a little Dutch girl in Grand Rapids, Michigan, "The Little Hero of Holland." Hague's illustrations of Peter, the Dutch boy who held his finger in the dike to save his country from flooding, make the story come alive. Be sure to notice the great windmills and wooden shoes.

Bishop, Claire, and Kurt Wiese. *Five Chinese Brothers.* Putnam, 1988.

You probably remember this one from your own childhood. Five Chinese brothers have amazing powers and use them to save their first brother's life.

Burton, Virginia Lee. *Mike Mulligan and His Steam Shovel.* Houghton Mifflin, 1939.

Mike Mulligan and his steam shovel, Mary Anne, should be introduced to every child. The author had a keen respect for the mind of a child and many of her stories are well-loved classics: *Katy and the Big Snow* and *The Little House* (winner of the Caldecott Medal in 1943) are two.

Cannon, Janell. *Stellaluna.* Harcourt Brace, 1993.

There are plenty of picture books about bears, cats, dogs, and monkeys, but this is the first one that features bats. Realistic and even a little scary, this marvelous story will not only tell you more about fruit bats than you ever wanted to know but will also affirm the uniqueness of each of God's creatures. The illustrations, wonderful acrylics with colored pencils, are almost scientific in their detail. This is a well-told story with just the right touches of humor.

Carle, Eric. *The Very Hungry Caterpillar.* Puffin, 1984.

Carle is a most prolific author and illustrator with dozens of titles to his credit. Even the most reluctant reader will become involved with Eric Carle's books. In this classic, the very hungry caterpillar eats his way through all kinds of fruit, leaving holes in the pages for curious fingers. Other Carle books have different engaging surprises not found in the typical read-aloud. There's not room to list all of his titles here but look for *The Mixed-Up Chameleon, The Secret Birthday Message, The Grouchy Ladybug,* and *The Greedy Python.*

Clark, Ann Nolan. *In My Mother's House.* Illustrated by Velino Herrara. Puffin, 1992.

Ann Nolan Clark has assembled a unique collection of poems written by Pueblo Indian children of New Mexico. It was one of the first books written (1941) from a Native American perspective. If you're traveling through the Southwest, be sure to take this book along as a read-aloud.

Cohen, Miriam. *When Will I Read?* Illustrated by Lillian Hoban. Greenwillow, 1977.

The author has a knack for describing the anxieties that beset the average first grader. She reassures children that they are special and that they can do it. Other stories in the same vein are *First Grade Takes a Test, Lost in the Museum, Will I Have a Friend?* and *No Good in Art.*

Coles, Robert. *The Story of Ruby Bridges.* Illustrated by George Ford. Scholastic Professional, 1995.

This true story of a child's courage and strength in the face of anger, prejudice, and hatred will move you. Ruby Bridges entered a whites-only school in New Orleans in 1960 and for months was the only black student in the entire school. With a dignity and faith belying her young years, she entered school each day praying for the angry crowd that lined the school walks. This is an important part of our history to share with your children.

De Brunhoff, Jean. *The Story of Babar, the Little Elephant.* Random House, 1961.

Babar is a rather sophisticated French elephant whose culture may well rub off on your children. The books have been translated from the French and the titles number over two dozen.

De Regniers, Beatrice Schenk. *May I Bring a Friend?* Atheneum, 1971.

A young boy is invited to tea with the king and queen but wants to bring a friend. He brings a giraffe and is naturally invited back for several other dining engagements. The boy returns each time with a new animal friend, and as the story ends we find the king and queen being feted with tea at the local zoo. A wonderful rhyme makes this a story that is easily memorized and read together.

Flack, Marjorie. *Angus and the Ducks.* Farrar, Straus and Giroux, 1997.

Angus is a curious Scottie dog who manages to escape from the house to explore the world. His encounter with a flock of ducks will give you ample opportunity for sound effects and dramatic interpretation. His curiosity also extends to cats in *Angus and the Cat* and fellow dogs in *Angus and the Dog*. This book was originally published in 1930, and you'll be glad that it's still around for your children to enjoy.

Graham, Ruth Bell. *One Wintry Night.* Illustrated by Richard Jesse Watson. Baker, 1994.

This is an absolutely stunning book. Ruth Bell Graham's retelling of the Christmas story—beginning with creation and concluding with the resurrection—is masterful. She writes with a simple eloquence that will hold both you and your children spellbound. Richard Jesse Watson's illustrations are beautifully rendered with an attention to color, detail, and sensitivity that is uncommon. The paper, binding, and design of this book enhance the story even more. You'll want two copies of this book one to regularly read aloud and another to collect. Take several days to read this one aloud; it's perfect for reading to the whole family.

Gramatky, Hardie. *Little Toot.* Putnam, 1992.

This is the well-told and oft-read tale of a little tugboat who has a hard time living up to the expectations of his Father and Grandfather Toot. Other titles by the same author are *Hercules, Loopy, Sparky, Little Toot on the Thames,* and *Little Toot on the Grand Canal.*

Higgs, Liz Curtis. *The Parable of the Pumpkin Patch.* Illustrated by Nancy Munger. Thomas Nelson, 1995.

A gentle story of planting, growing, and transformation, this book is a nice alternative to the usual goblins and witches of the fall season. Another story in a similar vein is *The Parable of the Lily.*

Hoban, Russell. *Bread and Jam for Frances.* Illustrated by Lillian Hoban. Harper and Row, 1964.

Frances is one of the most enchanting of all animal characters in children's literature and my own personal favorite. This independent-minded badger will win your heart as she refuses to eat anything but bread and jam. Mother Badger uses a bit of clever psychology on Frances, and soon Frances is begging for more variety in her menu. Other titles are *A Baby Sister for Frances, Bedtime for Frances, Best Friends for Frances, A Birthday for Frances,* and *A Bargain for Frances.*

Hunt, Angela Elwell. *The Tale of Three Trees.* Illustrated by Tim Jonke. Lion, 1989.

A beautiful retelling of an American folktale about three trees that are used in surprising ways—one to become the manger that holds the Christ Child, another a fishing boat to carry Jesus, and the third the cross on which Jesus is crucified. The illustrations are lush and set a worshipful tone for the story.

Hutchins, Pat. *Don't Forget the Bacon.* William Morrow, 1987.

Although the text is simple, don't be fooled; the humor is anything but. Your four to seven year old will enjoy how the main character tries to remember his mother's shopping list and ends up forgetting the bacon. I adore Pat Hutchins's stories, illustrations, and sense of humor. Other titles include *The Wind Blew, Clocks and More Clocks, The Surprise Party,* and *Titch.*

Joslin, Mary. *The Good Man of Assisi.* Illustrated by Allison Wisenfeld. Tommy Nelson, 1998.

This is an elegant account of the life of St. Francis of Assisi. He is a little-known person whose deep faith and care for all of God's creatures will be attractive to children.

Keats, Ezra Jack. *A Letter to Amy.* Harper and Row, 1968.

Ezra Jack Keats is famous for his collage illustrations, which you'll enjoy looking at almost as much as reading the simple story. The main character, Peter, who is featured in other Keats stories, invites a neighborhood girl to his birthday party. Other titles include *A Whistle for Willie, Peter's Chair,* and *The Snowy Day.*

Kellogg, Steven. *The Mystery of the Missing Red Mitten.* Dial, 1974.

If your child has ever lost a mitten, she will identify with Annie, who has lost five this winter. Together you will explore many possibilities for where the mitten might be, before finding it used as the heart of a melting snowman. Kellogg is a wonderful author and illustrator with an uncommon understanding of the mind of a child. You will not go wrong with any of his stories. Among the choices are *The Mysterious Tadpole, Can I Keep Him?* and *Much Bigger than Martin.*

Kraus, Robert. *Whose Mouse Are You?* Illustrated by Jose Aruego. Simon and Schuster, 1970.

Little Mouse is trying to figure out how he fits into his family, one that is no doubt similar to yours. My children and the hundreds to whom I've read Kraus's books aloud have loved both the illustrations and simple truths in all of these titles: *Leo the Late Bloomer* (for parents who wonder when their child will finally "bloom"); *Where Are You Going, Little Mouse?; Another Mouse to Feed;* and *Milton the Early Riser.*

Ladwig, Tim. *Psalm 23.* African American Family Press, 1993.

This book is a visual delight with twenty-four original full-color paintings that interpret Psalm 23 in the context of life in the inner city. Ladwig's renderings will speak to your heart as you reflect on how timely King David's ancient words are for the contemporary child and family.

Lionni, Leo. *Alexander and the Wind-Up Mouse.* Pantheon, 1969.

You will want to read all of the Leo Lionni books aloud. Not only are the stories filled with positive values, but Lionni's illustrations are works of art. Alexander the wind-up mouse is changed into a real mouse by a friend who wants to save his life. Look for these other titles: *Inch by Inch, Swimmy,* and *Fish Is Fish.*

Lucado, Max. *The Crippled Lamb.* Illustrated by Liz Bonham. Word, 1994.

Joshua, the crippled lamb, is used by God to help keep baby Jesus warm. This is a wonderful story of encouragement and inspiration to all of us who despair of finding a place where we can fit in. Lucado is a prolific author; you and your children will enjoy the message of his stories as well as the varied illustrators with whom he has teamed. Also look for *Tell Me a Story* and *You Are Special.*

McCloskey, Robert. *Make Way for Ducklings.* Viking, 1941.

This timeless story from your own childhood tells of how Mr. and Mrs. Mallard manage to raise their family of ducklings in the middle of Boston. Other McCloskey classics are *Blueberries for Sal, One Morning in Maine,* and *Lentil.*

Marshall, James. *George and Martha.* Houghton Mifflin, 1973.

Each George and Martha book has five ministories about two engaging hippos. Animals who act like humans are a favorite source of material for children's authors, and Marshall is especially skilled at creating vignettes that capture the relationship between good friends. Look for *George and Martha Encore, George and Martha Back in Town, George and Martha Tons of Fun, George and Martha One Fine Day,* and *George and Martha Rise and Shine.*

Milne, A. A. *Winnie-the-Pooh.* Illustrated by E. H. Shepard. E. P. Dutton, 1926.

Winnie-the-Pooh is not strictly a picture book, since the original illustrations are small line drawings and the book numbers over 150 pages. However, the chapters are self-contained short stories that need not be read consecutively. Every child should meet the original Christopher Robin, Winnie-the-Pooh, Eeyore, Little Roo, Rabbit, Owl, and Kanga before being spoiled by the Disney versions. These are characters in children's literature with remarkable freshness and charm. Other titles by the author are *The World of Christopher Robin, The Pooh Song Book,* and *Pooh's Birthday Book.*

Munger, Robert Boyd, with Carolyn Nystrom. *My Heart–Christ's Home: Retold for Children.* Illustrated by Jerry Tiritilli. InterVarsity Press, 1997.

Ten million copies of the pamphlet "My Heart—Christ's Home" by Robert Boyd Munger have been distributed by InterVarsity Press. Now Carolyn Nystrom and Jerry Tiritilli have adapted Munger's message in a beautiful picture book for reading aloud. You will read this story dozens of times and still not absorb all of the beauty and meaning that is there.

Pienkowski, Jan. *Easter.* A. A. Knopf, 1989.

Pienkowski is a master illustrator, and his interpretation of the Easter story using the King James translation is sure to become a tradition at your house. Pienkowski uses silhouetting, brilliant color, and sumptuous ornamental gilding to create a collector's item.

Rey, H. A. *Curious George.* Houghton Mifflin, 1941.

There is something endearing about this curious monkey, most likely because of his ingenious ability to outwit nearly every human he meets. Read all of the Curious George titles: *Curious George Takes a Job, Curious George Rides a Bike, Curious George Gets a Medal, Curious George Flies a Kite, Curious George Learns the Alphabet,* and *Curious George Goes to the Hospital.*

Seuss, Dr. *The Five Hundred Hats of Bartholomew Cubbins.* Vanguard, 1938.

Dr. Seuss has two types of stories for children—easy to read, controlled vocabulary stories (see entry under Independent Readers) and full-length read-alouds. Be prepared to read them over and over, because children delight in the tongue twisters, imaginative rhymes, and alliteration, and they love his illustrations. Some other Seuss favorites are *And to Think That I Saw It on Mulberry Street, How the Grinch Stole Christmas, Horton Hatches the Egg, Horton Hears a Who, McElligot's Pool,* and *Yertle the Turtle.*

Slobodkina, Esphyr. *Caps for Sale.* HarperCollins Juvenile, 1988.

This timeless story of "a peddler, some monkeys, and their monkey business" is surprisingly fresh in its illustrations and text despite the fact that it will soon celebrate its fiftieth birthday.

Waber, Bernard. *Ira Sleeps Over.* Houghton Mifflin, 1979.

Ira can hardly wait to sleep over at his best friend's house. Naturally he plans to take along his teddy bear until his older sister ridicules the plan. When he discovers his friend Reggie has a beloved bear called Foo Foo, Ira returns home to get his own beloved Tah Tah. Also by Bernard Waber: *Lyle, Lyle Crocodile, Lyle and the Birthday Party,* and *The House on East 88th Street.*

Wells, Rosemary. *Moss Pillows: A Voyage to the Bunny Planet.* Dial Books for Young Readers, 1992.

This book is one of three titles in *The Bunny Planet* series: *First Tomato* and *The Island Light* are the others. The Bunny Planet is where Wells's lovable characters go when they've had a bad day. There they experience the day that should have been. All of us need our own version of the Bunny Planet. How fortunate for your child that Rosemary Wells discovered this celestial body in the nick of time.

Wildsmith, Brian. *Joseph.* Eerdmans Books for Young Readers, 1997.

A lush interpretation of the favorite Bible story about Joseph and his coat of many colors, this is Wildsmith at his finest. Purchase this book for your child's collection.

Willard, Nancy. *The High Rise Glorious Skittle Skat Roarious Sky Pie Angel Food Cake.* Illustrated by Richard Jesse Watson. Voyager Picture Books, 1996.

This isn't your average read-aloud but it's certainly a winner and is a Caldecott Honor Book. It defies classification by the average librarian. Some call it a picture book for four to eight year olds and others classify it as children's fiction for older children. It's the entrancing story of a young girl who sets out to find an heirloom recipe for High Rise Glorious Skittle Skat Roarious Sky Pie Angel Food Cake so she can give her mother the only thing she wants for her birthday. The youthful baker is visited by angels who help her create a truly heavenly cake. The text is wonderfully written and the illustrations by Watson are works of art. Some families have made this heavenly cake a birthday tradition at their house after reading the story.

Yolen, Jane. *Owl Moon.* Illustrated by John Schoenherr. Philomel, 1987.

This magical tale of a child's walk through the wintry woods with her father to hunt for the great horned owl won the Caldecott Award in 1988. The pictures evoke New England, the north woods, or anyplace with majestic pines and snow that is "whiter than the milk in a cereal bowl." You'll shiver in the evening chill, and the excitement is almost palpable when Pa turns on his big flashlight and you stare into the owl's eyes. To every person who has enjoyed a special grown-up time with a father, this book will evoke powerful emotions. Another magical book by Yolen, this one illustrated by Ed Young, is *The Emperor and the Kite*, a story about the Chinese emperor's youngest daughter, who rescues her father from prison by flying her kite.

Young, Ed. *Seven Blind Mice.* Philomel, 1992.

Although at first glance this would appear to be a simple picture book, you will find Ed Young's award-winning retelling of the ancient fable of the blind men and the elephant to be rather sophisticated in both concept and moral. This book is worth purchasing.

Zion, Gene. *Harry the Dirty Dog.* Illustrated by Margaret Bloy Graham. Harper and Row, 1956.

Harry is a dog that everyone loves. His adventures are funny but, most important, believable. Every child wishes that Harry could be their dog. Other titles include

Harry by the Sea, No Roses for Harry, and *Harry and the Lady Next Door.*

Zolotow, Charlotte. *William's Doll.* Illustrated by William Pene Du Bois. Harper and Row, 1972.

Charlotte Zolotow has collaborated with a variety of outstanding illustrators (Maurice Sendak, Garth Williams, Leonard Weisgard, and Kay Chorao) to create many wonderful picture books, each with a different style and type of story. The sentiments expressed in *William's Doll* should touch the heart of every father. William wants a doll and only his grandmother understands why that might be important. There are over fifty Zolotow titles to choose from. Other favorites are *Mr. Rabbit and the Lovely Present, Do You Know What I'll Do? My Friend John, My Grandson Lew,* and *Hold My Hand.*

Books for the Independent Reader

The books in this category will serve two purposes—they can be read aloud to your child, but more important, your child will eventually read them on her own. These are well-written stories your beginner can read independently once she has learned how the alphabetic code works, in other words, phonics.

Beware of letting your children make the mistake of thinking that when they have memorized a predictable book, they are actually reading. They will not be able to memorize every word of every book and will eventually need to understand that good readers decode the words they read; they only memorize those words that can't be decoded (sight words). I've heard tell of beginning readers who have assured parents and teachers, "I don't have to read it; I already know it." This trick will work for a while, especially with bright children, but then the sheer quantity of reading material will overwhelm the student who is relying only on memory.

To become fluent readers, beginners need to practice with books that give them a high degree of success; 95 percent is the recommended rate. They also need to read a word successfully fourteen to eighteen times before it becomes a part of their automatic reading vocabulary.

Easy readers have certain characteristics that make them unmistakable: short and simple stories, large type, and a controlled vocabulary. Once a child has learned a certain set of sounds, finding material for practice that contains these sounds is crucial. Your child needs to be able to sound out words on her own, rather than guessing. Consult resource H for a list of titles that contain repetitions of the various vowel sounds your child will need to learn and practice. As your child gains skill with simple readers on her own, continue to read aloud a wide variety of more challenging picture books, fairy tales, and poetry so that she can experience the richness of the English language, gain knowledge, and stretch her thinking and comprehension skills. While she is learning how to decode and make sense of the printed word on her own, she needs the stimulation that more difficult read aloud children's literature will bring.

Space limitations do not permit me to list the hundreds of wonderful early reading books that are available; I've included just a few of my (and my children's) personal favorites, but if you are eager to find more titles, consult the excellent book *Beyond Picture Books*,[1] which contains annotated lists of over one thousand early readers. Many of the books have been given a grade level label based on their difficulty. If this book is not in your local public library, suggest to the children's librarian that it be purchased as a reference for parents and used as a guideline for purchasing easy reading books for the library's collection.

Benchley, Nathaniel. *Sam the Minuteman.* Illustrated by Arnold Lobel. Harper-Collins, 1987.

If your child enjoys adventure stories about real people, Nathaniel Benchley provides them in his beginning reader books. He brings the Revolutionary War to life through the eyes of *Sam the Minuteman* and *George the Drummer Boy* (other Benchley titles). Others include *Oscar Otter, The Strange Disappearance of Arthur Cluck,* and *Red Fox and His Canoe.*

Eastman, P. D. *Go, Dog, Go!* Random House Childrens, 1961.

The covers of this book were taped together on more than one occasion at our house. The repetition of easily decodable words and short sentences will give your beginning reader confidence in her ability to read independently. Somehow a party of wild dogs on top of a tree will not seem too improbable after the fortieth or fiftieth reading of this favorite.

Hoban, Lillian. *Arthur's Pen Pal.* HarperCollins, 1987.

Arthur and Violet are a charming brother-sister pair of chimpanzees that experience plenty of sibling rivalry along the way to working out their problems. The messages of loving, sharing, and caring come through loud and clear. There are many titles, some of them with cassettes, with which your children can enjoy reading along: *Arthur's Honey Bear, Arthur's Back to School Day, Arthur's Campout, Arthur's Christmas Cookies, Arthur's Funny Money,* and *Arthur's Halloween Costume.*

Lobel, Arnold. *Small Pig.* Harper and Row, 1969.

This title numbers among the favorites of my children. Small Pig is an endearing character who leaves the farm because the farmer's wife has a penchant for cleanliness. Lobel is a master at writing easy-to-read but interesting and well-plotted stories. His *Frog and Toad* series should not be missed. You and your children will love the remarkable relationship between these two animals. My favorite is *Frog and Toad Are Friends.* Another title by Lobel is *Owl at Home.*

Minarik, Elsa H. *Little Bear's Visit.* Illustrated by Maurice Sendak. Harper and Row, 1961.

> *Little Bear* is another beginning reader series that is special. The gift of telling a beautiful story in few and simple words has been bestowed on Elsa Minarik, and Sendak's illustrations are an added bonus. Your children will be the benefactors of their gifts. Other titles are *Little Bear, Father Bear Comes Home, Little Bear's Friend, Little Bear's Visit,* and *A Kiss for Little Bear.* Read every one.

Parrish, Peggy. *Amelia Bedelia.* Illustrated by Fritz Siebel. HarperCollins Juvenile, 1992.

> Amelia Bedelia is an intrepid housekeeper/nanny who takes everything literally. Children will delight as she follows all of her employer's instructions to the letter. Look for every Amelia Bedelia title you can find: *Amelia Bedelia Helps Out, Amelia Bedelia and the Baby, Amelia Bedelia and Her Wacky World,* and *Amelia Bedelia and the Surprise Shower.*

Seuss, Dr. *One Fish, Two Fish, Red Fish, Blue Fish.* Random House, 1960.

> No one has a way with words like Dr. Seuss. He puts them together in a rhyming fashion that captivates children. His drawings won't win any art awards, but kids don't care. They love the funny little characters and weird animals and they can read what he's written almost as easily as you can. There are dozens of titles but among the most popular are *The Cat in the Hat; The Cat in the Hat Comes Back; Marvin K. Mooney, Will You Please Go Now; The Foot Book;* and *The Shape of Me and Other Stuff.* Others by Dr. Seuss under a different name (Theo. LeSieg) are *In a People House; Hooper Humperdink? Not Him!* and *Ten Apples Up on Top.*

Sharmat, Marjorie Weinman. *Nate the Great and the Missing Key.* Young Yearling, 1982.

> If your child enjoys solving a mystery, this series will challenge her thinking skills. Look for these other Nate

the Great titles: *Nate the Great and the Fishy Prize, Nate the Great and the Lost List, Nate Goes Undercover, Nate the Great and the Phony Clue, Nate the Great and the Snowy Trail, Nate the Great and the Musical Note,* and *Nate the Great and the Sticky Case.*

Concept, Counting, and Alphabet Books for the Older Child

The books in this category are written for the older child. They demand a more sophisticated reader and teach more complex skills. They are an important source of continuing learning for your child.

Elting, Mary, and Michael Folsom. *Q Is for Duck: An Alphabet Guessing Game.* Illustrated by Jack Kent. Houghton Mifflin, 1980.

This alphabet book calls for quick thinking. The reader has to figure out why *A* is for zoo, *B* is for dog, and *C* is for hen. The illustrations are colorful and lively.

Johnson, Stephen T. *Alphabet City.* New York: Viking Childrens Books, 1996.

Who says alphabet books are for little kids? This one may challenge even you. The stunning paintings in a variety of media capture urban scenes in which each of the letters of the alphabet can be found, albeit tucked away in unusual places. Is this an alphabet book, an art book, or a treasure hunt? It all depends on how you read it. You and your child will have hours of fun.

Kitchen, Bert. *Animal Alphabet.* Penguin USA, 1992.

This alphabet book is a work of art. The author has created stunning animal paintings that interweave with full-page block letters. The reader must guess the animal names, but for many of those featured you will need to consult the answer page found in the back of the book. Among the more unusual are quetzal, vulture, x-ray fish, and jerboa. This alphabet book is for the child who appreciates the unusual.

Shannon, George. *Tomorrow's Alphabet.* Illustrated by Donald Crews. Greenwillow, 1996.

> A unique alphabet book that expects children to make the leap from today into tomorrow when confronted with a letter and word—*T* is for bread, tomorrow's toast; *K* is for tomato, tomorrow's ketchup. Well, you get the idea. And so will your children.

Folk and Fairy Tales

Folk and fairy tales continue to be an important source of literary challenge for the child. The most eminent Christian writers of fantasy like J. R. R. Tolkien and C. S. Lewis praised the fairy tale for its richness and ability to expand our thinking. Reading the classic fairy tales to your children will exercise their imaginations, expand their language and concept development, reinforce timeless lessons and morals, and open limitless possibilities for creativity.

Aesop, editor. *Aesop's Fables.* Illustrated by Safaya Salter. Harcourt Brace, 1992.

> You'll find many of your old favorites, such as "The Fox and the Crow" and "The Tortoise and Hare," as well as some more unfamiliar ones in this volume. The illustrations are in an eastern Mediterranean style with jewel-like colors and rich page borders.

Brown, Marcia. *Stone Soup.* C. Scribner's, 1989.

> Marcia Brown specializes in the interpretation of fairy tales and has won several Caldecott awards for her work. How do three hungry soldiers trick an entire village into donating vegetables and beef to make soup from a stone? Read this one aloud to find out. Other favorite tales interpreted by Brown include *Once a Mouse, Cinderella, Puss in Boots, Dick Whittington and His Cat,* and *The Steadfast Tin Soldier.*

dePaola, Tomie. *Favorite Nursery Tales.* Putnam, 1986.

This volume is a collection of well-loved favorite fairy tales that every child should know—cultural literacy for kids, if you will. The author selected his favorites from childhood, and they will become your child's favorites as well.

dePaola, Tomie. *Strega Nona: An Old Tale.* Simon and Schuster, 1989.

This author has done extensive research into folktales, and his illustrations have an unmistakable charm. This Italian folktale centers around a magic pasta pot. Other dePaola titles are *The Prince of the Dolomites* and *The Clown of God.*

Galdone, Paul. *The Gingerbread Boy.* Houghton Mifflin, 1975.

Galdone does a masterful job of interpreting the best folk and fairy tales. His illustrations have a whimsy that brings new life to familiar stories. Sample them all: *The Little Red Hen, The Three Bears, The Three Billy Goats Gruff, The Magic Porridge Pot, Henny Penny, Little Tuppen,* and *Old Mother Hubbard and Her Dog.*

Ginsburg, Mirra. *Mushroom in the Rain.* Illustrated by Jose Aruego and Ariane Dewey. Demco Media, 1990.

How can so many animals hide under one mushroom? The wise old frog explains—it's rain that makes the mushroom grow. Also look for *Where Does the Sun Go at Night?*

Green, Norma. *The Hole in the Dike.* Illustrated by Eric Carle. Thomas Y. Crowell, 1974.

Green retells the story about a courageous Dutch boy who holds his finger in the dike to save his village from flooding. The illustrations are vintage Carle.

Hogrogian, Nonny. *One Fine Day.* Aladdin Paperbacks, 1986.

This African folktale is a great read-aloud. A greedy fox learns that what is taken must be replaced.

Hyman, Trina Schart. *Little Red Riding Hood.* Holiday House, 1983.

Reviewers have called this illustrator's interpretation of the familiar fairy tales "romantic, lush, and mysterious."

This retelling of "Little Red Riding Hood" has some humorous touches as well. As the heroine of our story leaves her grandmother's house after barely escaping from her adventure with the wolf, she comforts herself with the thought that at least she minded her manners. Hyman has illustrated other folktales: *Snow White, The Sleeping Beauty,* and *Rapunzel.*

Kipling, Rudyard. *Just So Stories.* Illustrated by Barry Moser. William Morrow, 1996.

If you want to find out how the leopard really got his spots and how the camel really got his hump, check out these far-fetched explanations concocted by Rudyard Kipling. Although this title is categorized as Young Adult in some listings, my experience is that unless you expose your children to these stories when they're young, you'll never get them even to consider Kipling when they're young adults.

Mosel, Arlene. *Tikki, Tikki, Tembo.* Illustrated by Blair Lent. Henry Holt, 1988.

Legend has it that the first and honored Chinese sons were always given very long names. This folktale tells how that custom was changed. Another folktale by Mosel is *The Funny Little Woman.*

Tresselt, Alvin. *The Mitten: An Old Ukrainian Folktale.* Mulberry, 1989.

I've read this retelling of a Ukrainian folktale to hundreds of children over the years and I never grow tired of hearing it again. Children are intrigued by the idea of a mouse, frog, owl, rabbit, fox, wolf, boar, and bear settling in for the winter in a lost mitten.

Poetry

The poetry collections mentioned in chapter 3 will serve you very nicely as your children mature. In addition, the following volumes are definitely appealing to older readers.

Hopkins, Lee Bennett. *Surprises.* Illustrated by Megan Lloyd. HarperCollins, 1986.

Poems that beginning readers can handle on their own have been collected by Lee Bennett Hopkins. This small volume is even indexed. Hooray!

O'Neill, Mary. *Hailstones and Halibut Bones: Adventures in Color.* Illustrated by John Wallner. Doubleday, 1990.

This classic from the '60s was reissued with lush full-color illustrations, one for each of the twelve poems and twelve colors. The colors of the spectrum come alive.

Prelutsky, Jack. *For Laughing Out Loud: Poems to Tickle Your Funnybone.* Illustrated by Marjorie Priceman. A. A. Knopf, 1991.

If Robert Louis Stevenson and A. A. Milne are too tame for your tastes, then try this humorous collection of poems. Once you start reading, you may not want to share the book with your child.

CHAPTER Five

The Middle Grades

Ages 8 to 12

• • •

> No book is really worth reading at the age of ten which is not equally (and often far more) worth reading at the age of fifty.
>
> C. S. Lewis

'Ve never understood parents who bemoan the passing of their children into the middle grades. To me, this period of time offered the best of all possible worlds. My children were toilet trained and independent, but they weren't driving cars yet. Most exciting to me as a librarian and educator was the fact that they loved to talk about what they were reading. They had opinions about everything. Unable to keep up with the avalanche of new children's books that came pouring into the school library where I worked, I tapped their expertise as book reviewers. We spent many evenings discussing just which books were good and why. Many of the suggestions that follow come from our experiences together as a family.

The years between the ages of eight and twelve will find your child exploring a variety of social relationships. The children you will meet in the section ahead are concerned about friends, fitting in the group, and being accepted. They like to read about young people their own age meeting the challenges of growing up, whether in this century, the last, or in some future time or space. Perhaps you'll recognize your own child among the group I describe. Later in the chapter you will find out which books are especially recommended for reading aloud to young people in this age category.

The Children

Joe is eight years old. One of the most important people in his life right now is his new best friend, Mark. The two boys spend hours together making models. Joe is a collector of so many different things that his mother despairs of cleaning his room. Matchbook covers, dinosaur models, comic books—his room looks like a garage sale.

Joe is an excellent independent reader but still enjoys having other family members read aloud to him. His favorites so far are *Charlotte's Web* and *James and the Giant Peach*. His mom is an important person in his life, and he is jealous of the time she spends at her work and with other family members. When they're home together, Joe follows her around the house like a shadow.

Joe likes school and is eager to talk with his family about what happens there. He also enjoys Sunday school. He is extremely interested in Bible stories and is beginning to memorize short passages of Scripture. His membership in Awana Club is important to him and he eagerly prepares for the badge tests. He says his prayers with regularity each night and still wants a bedtime story.

The most tiresome aspect of Joe's personality is his readiness to engage in arguments. He is especially rude to his grandmother, who lives with the family, and is often sent to his room for losing his temper. But he never broods long over these temporary tempests and is usually willing to apologize. Joe is both a delight and a challenge to his parents.

Samantha is ten years old and in fifth grade. She comes forth with penetratingly accurate descriptions and imitations of teachers and family friends. Her insights and outspokenness frequently embarrass her parents. She desperately wants to be thought of as grown-up, and there are frequent disagreements over what kind of clothing is most appropriate for a ten year old.

School is important to Samantha. She likes her teacher because she's fair, a quality that is extremely important to the average fifth grader. Samantha's life is filled with activities from morning till night—reading, drawing, playing with her doll collection, practicing piano lessons, writing to Grandma, or just being with friends.

Samantha is a willing helper but needs frequent reminders to actually follow through on her jobs. Often preoccupied with her own activities, she sometimes doesn't bother to answer when called. This trait causes some friction between Mom and Samantha.

Samantha loves tales of make-believe and fantasy. Her favorite read-alouds are *Tales of the Kingdom* and *The Chronicles of Narnia*. Although she loves to read aloud favorite books from her own early years to her younger siblings, she prefers reading more difficult books on her own. She is an avid reader and won the One-Hundred Book Club award at school.

Part of her busy social schedule each week is attendance at Pioneer Girls. Samantha is diligently earning badges and working on projects. Several girls from school attend with her and this makes going twice as much fun. Samantha also is a regular user of the church library. She loves to read about girls who are slightly older and encountering grown-up problems with boys and dates. Samantha is eagerly looking forward to growing up.

Dylan is twelve years old, a most glorious age according to his mother. He tinkers with old appliances around the house and last week reassembled a broken toaster with great success. He was able to help cook dinner when his mom had the flu. And only last week his teacher called with an excellent report on what was happening in school.

Dylan is on the threshold of adolescence and already his parents can see the young man he will become. His sensitive insight into people and their needs was evident when Dylan befriended a new boy in school that others were ridiculing. He takes the lessons he learns in Sunday school and family devotions very seriously and often reminds other members of his family of their responsibilities. Dylan loves to read about boys facing real-life danger where good triumphs over evil. His favorites include *The Spirit Flyer* series. He has many contemporary heroes in the sports world and is an avid football and baseball fan. Dylan became a Christian during summer camp and is eager to read about real boys and girls encountering tests of their Christian faith in everyday life.

His best friend lives just down the street; Dylan and Matt are inseparable. They frequently sleep over, exchange computer games, and work on school projects together. But Dylan still manages to find time to shoot baskets with his older brother. His parents are enjoying this period of relative calm in Dylan's life and are using his interest and responsiveness to build a relationship that will carry them through the storms of adolescence.

The Choices

The choices from which to make your read aloud selections will be grouped in the following categories: Bible story books and Bible translations; read aloud novels; poetry; classics; anthologies of children's literature; and legends, myths, folk and fairy tales.

Bible Story Books and Bible Translations

Some have suggested that Bible reading be looked on as "dessert" after dinner in the evening. Becky Slough, a children's bookseller in Illinois, has set forth a number of excellent ideas for using the Bible as a read-aloud. She suggests that parents allow the Holy Spirit to be the primary instructive agent and concentrate on reading the passages in the best possible way with little comment. I concur, having grown up in a home where dessert and the Bible were served up together. There were never sermons or lectures, only the reading of the Word. We started at Genesis and read to Revelation. Only when we reached the Song of Solomon did we skip on to the next book. My father assured us that this book was better read silently.

The Bible can be shared with children of this age in two ways: Bible story books and translations. A Bible story book retells the favorite Bible stories. The author brings his or her own interpretation to the retelling, and the author's choice of words dictates the complexity and level of sophistication. A translation is the work of a group of scholars laboring over Hebrew and Greek texts, desiring to be quite exacting in their choice of words and phrases.

Batchelor, Mary. *The Children's Bible in 365 Stories.* Illustrated by John Haysom. Chariot Victor, 1995.

> A finalist in the Gold Medallion Book Awards, this version has a read aloud story for every day of the year. Illustrations are of the highest quality and the stories are well written. Included are parts of the Bible not often covered in a Bible story anthology, like Proverbs, Psalms, the Prophets, and New Testament letters.

Briscoe, Jill and Stuart. *Moses Takes a Road Trip and Other Famous Journeys.* Illustrated by Russ Flint. Baker, 1996.

> It's hard to categorize this book since it's more than a Bible story book. It contains a little bit of everything: well written and illustrated Bible stories, songs, games, some good old-fashioned "just pretend" stories, activities, and the "factoids" that kids enjoy so much. This is the kind of book you'll sample depending on the mood and occasion, but your children will never complain about "boring" Bible stories again. Other titles in the series include *Jesus Makes a Major Comeback and Other Amazing Feats, David Drops a Giant Problem and Other Fearless Heroes,* and *Paul Hits the Beach and Other Wild Adventures.*

Holy Bible, Children's New Living Translation. Tyndale, 1997.

> This is an ideal choice for a child's first Bible. It contains sixteen pages of full-color illustrations, a dictionary/concordance, and fifty-two in-text life application notes with memory verses.

Kids' Life Application Bible. Tyndale, 1998.

> The *Kids Life Application Bible* is based on the text of the New Living Translation and contains a number of special features such as Heroes and Villains (notes describing good and bad Bible people to help kids learn valuable lessons), I Wonder (notes explaining difficult concepts and answers to questions kids have about the Bible), and Sticky Situations (short stories in which kids are asked to make a decision with moral implications).

Taylor, Kenneth N. *Living Bible Story Book.* Tyndale, 1985.

> Seventy-three brief Bible stories are included along with seventy-five full-color illustrations by Richard and Frances Hook.

The Rock. Tyndale, 1998.

> Based on the New Living Translation, this Bible for pre-teens and teens emphasizes decision making about critical contemporary issues like AIDS, premarital sex, abortion, and the use of money. A unique feature is "People at the Crossroads," which contains profiles of Bible people who made moral decisions both good and bad.

Read Aloud Novels

The read aloud novels in this section are chapter books that will take an extended period of time to complete. You may choose to read a chapter per evening or read lengthier sections while taking a car trip. Some families prefer to use books on tape to enhance the listening experience while driving, especially if motion sickness is a problem. Many of the recommended titles have been produced as cassettes.

The titles are from four categories: fantasy, realistic fiction, biography, and historical fiction. Expose your child to all four. Once you begin a book, your only difficulty will be in suspending your reading until the next read aloud session. When your children begin borrowing the book to read ahead on their own, you will know that they are hooked on books.

Alexander, Lloyd. *The Book of Three.* Dell, 1978.

> *The Chronicles of Prydain* is a five-volume series of which this title is the first. Based on Welsh mythology, the books tell the story of Taran, the assistant pig keeper, who with his band of companions defeats the forces of evil to become the high king. The five volumes tell a continuing story with each successive book written at a more difficult reading level. Here are the remaining titles in chronological order: *The Black Cauldron, The Castle of Llyr, Taran Wanderer,* and *The High King.*

Bibee, John. *Magic Bicycle.* InterVarsity Press, 1983.

Bibee produces creative yet believable adventures that are resolved in a fantasy world that clearly delineates good and evil. God's grace and forgiveness are communicated in graphic and unmistakable ways. The magic bicycle of the title is actually a rusty old Spirit Flyer model found in the city dump. It surprises its new owner, John Kramar, when it magically lives up to its name. Other titles in *The Spirit Flyer* series include *Bicycle Hills: How One Halloween Almost Got Out of Hand; The Only Game in Town; The Perfect Star: Becoming Children of the True King;* and *The Runaway Parents: The Parable of the Problem Parents.*

Bond, Michael. *A Bear Called Paddington.* Illustrated by Peggy Fortnum. Yearling, 1968.

Paddington, the endearing English bear named after the station in which he was found by the Brown family, has a special talent for getting into trouble; as one reviewer put it: "trouble sticks to Paddington like marmalade on toast." My children adored Paddington and yours will too.

Brink, Carol Ryrie. *Caddie Woodlawn.* Illustrated by Trina Schart Hyman. Aladdin Paperbacks, 1990.

This Newberry Award–winning book is about the frontier adventures of a tomboy, Caddie Woodlawn, drawn from the life of the author's grandmother's childhood. There's enough adventure in this book to entice even the most reluctant reader, especially if she happens to be a tomboy like Caddie.

Burnett, Frances Hodgson. *The Secret Garden.* Illustrated by Tasha Tudor. Bantam, 1987.

This story was my favorite as a child. I don't remember how many times I read it. I became Mary Lenox, the willful orphan girl who enters the secret garden to discover her uncle's invalid child. Lonely and without playmates growing up, I envied Mary's friendship with Colin through which she experiences the true joy of giving to others. This is a challenging read-aloud; the language is descriptive and rich. To give equal time to the male members of the family, read *Little Lord Fauntleroy,* the story of an American boy who goes to live with his grandfather in England and becomes heir to a title and fortune.

Burnford, Sheila. *The Incredible Journey.* Yearling, 1990.

A frisky young Labrador retriever, an aging bull terrier, and a Siamese cat set out on a two-hundred-mile journey through a wooded wilderness to return to their home. The adventures encountered by this intrepid trio make wonderful fireside reading.

Butterworth, Oliver. *The Enormous Egg.* Illustrated by Louis Darling. Little, Brown, 1993.

Twelve-year-old Nate Twitchell takes on the Washington establishment in an effort to save the dinosaur that hatched from an enormous egg. The theme has an amazing relevance to contemporary politics, even though it's been forty years since it was written.

Catling, Patrick Skene. *Chocolate Touch.* Dell, 1996.

John Midas will remind your middle grader of the mythical King Midas, whose touch turned everything to gold. John has a similar problem—everything he touches turns to chocolate. This story teaches a valuable lesson about greed and reads aloud very well.

Cleary, Beverly. *Ramona the Pest.* Camelot, 1996.

Life in the Quimby household is never dull when the youngest of the Quimby children, Ramona, is on stage. This volume follows Ramona through her kindergarten year. This series is a good one to read if your family read aloud session numbers children from several different age groups. Other books in the series are *Ramona and Her Father; Ramona the Brave; Ramona Quimby, Age Eight;* and

Ramona Forever. Cleary has written some other excellent read-alouds like *Dear Mr. Henshaw* and *The Mouse and the Motorcycle.*

Cooper, Susan. *Over Sea, Under Stone.* Harcourt Brace, 1988.

This is an amazing story that imaginative readers will love. Three English children on holiday in Cornwall with their Great-uncle Merry find King Arthur's Holy Grail. The ancient relic holds the power to fight the forces of evil. If your children enjoy C. S. Lewis and Tolkien, they'll be entranced by the battle between Light and Dark in *The Dark Is Rising* series by Cooper. Other titles are *Silver on the Tree, Greenwitch,* and *The Grey King.*

Dahl, Roald. *James and the Giant Peach.* Illustrated by Lane Smith. Puffin, 1996.

Dahl's gift is in making the ridiculous seem totally believable. You'll immediately be caught up in this fantasy of a boy who flies away in a giant peach with a cast of incredible characters. Other Dahl classics are *Charlie and the Chocolate Factory, Fantastic Mr. Fox,* and *Danny the Champion of the World.*

Dalgliesh, Alice. *The Courage of Sarah Noble.* Aladdin Paperbacks, 1991.

An eight-year-old girl finds the courage to go alone with her father to build a new home in the Connecticut wilderness and then to stay behind with the Indians when her father goes back to bring the rest of the family.

Fitzgerald, John D. *The Great Brain.* Illustrated by Mercer Mayer. Yearling, 1972.

This series was at the top of my son's list of favorites when he was growing up. The great brain is Tom Dennis. His brothers Sweyn and J. D. can scarcely keep up with the schemes he hatches in a small, turn-of-the-century Utah town. The adventures make for hilarious reading. Every child would like to be a part of this family and can be through the read aloud experience. Other Great Brain books are *The Great Brain at the Academy, The Great Brain Does It Again, The Great Brain Reforms,*

Me and My Little Brain, More Adventures of the Great Brain, and *Return of the Great Brain.*

Fox, Paula. *One-Eyed Cat.* Yearling, 1985.

The very moving story of a young boy who receives a rifle for Christmas from his uncle. Forbidden by his parents to touch it, he sneaks to the attic one night and uses it just once. Shooting at a shadow in the dark, he is unsure about what he has hit. His uncertainty turns to remorse when he sees a one-eyed wild cat prowling about his neighbor's yard. Convinced that he has shot out the cat's eye, Ned's life is beset with guilt and fear. This book will touch anyone who has lived with unconfessed sin.

Gates, Doris. *Blue Willow.* Viking, 1976.

This Newberry Honor Book (1940) is the timeless story of a child's desire for roots and friends. The child of a migrant worker, Janey Larkin treasures more than anything an heirloom plate with a blue and white Chinese pagoda willow pattern. Symbolic to her of permanence, she eventually makes the sacrifice of her life when she offers her precious plate to pay the rent.

George, Jean Craighead. *My Side of the Mountain.* Viking, 1991.

When I first read this Newberry Honor Book aloud to a fifth-grade class I was teaching, they were spellbound. Sam Gribley is a nature-loving boy who runs away to the woods and lives off the land. The adventurer in all of us can identify with Sam's resourcefulness.

Gipson, Fred. *Old Yeller.* Harper Trophy, 1990.

This title is a perennial read aloud favorite. Old Yeller is a big, ugly, yellow dog who showed up out of nowhere one night. Although Travis didn't much like Old Yeller in the beginning, he soon found he couldn't get along without him. Set during frontier days (late 1860s) in the Texas hill country, this is a moving and ultimately very sad story. Be prepared to shed a few tears.

Grahame, Kenneth. *The Wind in the Willows.* Illustrated by Michael Hague. Henry Holt, 1980.

There are dozens of versions of this timeless classic, but Michael Hague's illustrations make this one a collector's item. This book should definitely be read aloud! Children in the eight to twelve age group who will most enjoy and appreciate the plot and humor are frequently unable to manage the vocabulary on their own. Don't worry. Just read and let the context and flow of the story carry you along.

Hunkin, Oliver, editor. *Dangerous Journey: The Story of Pilgrim's Progress.* Illustrated by Alan Parry. Eerdmans, 1985.

This abridged edition of John Bunyan's *The Pilgrim's Progress* is a collector's item for the superb illustrations alone. You will enjoy the selections that have been adapted as well as the visual impact of the art.

Hunt, Irene. *Across Five Aprils.* Berkley, 1991.

When Jethro Creighton is given the responsibility to care for his family's farm in Illinois during the turbulent years of the Civil War, he quickly changes from a boy to a man. This is a challenging read-aloud, and you'll need to provide some historical background to make it come alive for your children.

Juster, Norton. *The Phantom Tollbooth.* Random House, 1993.

Be prepared for lots of unfamiliar words and more than a few puns. In the kingdom of Dictionopolis, reigned over by King AZAZ the Unabridged, a young boy named Milo encounters unabridged fun.

Konigsburg, E. L. *From the Mixed-Up Files of Mrs. Basil E. Frankweiler.* Yearling, 1977.

Children will identify with Claudia and her younger brother Jamie, two big-city kids who run away from home to take up residence in the Metropolitan Museum of Art. Once in the museum they are caught up in a mystery that adds suspense and excitement to the story. Konigsburg's other books are *Jennifer, Hecate, Macbeth, William McKinley, and Me, Elizabeth; About the B'nai Bagels; Altogether, One at a Time; A Proud Taste for Scarlet and Miniver; The Dragon in the Ghetto Caper; The Second Mrs. Giaconda;* and *Father's Arcane Daughter.*

Lawson, Robert. *Ben and Me.* Little, Brown, 1939.

In this timeless favorite of middle-grade children we find out that the real power behind Benjamin Franklin was a mouse named Amos. Stories with similar themes are *Mr. Revere and I* and *Captain Kidd's Cat.* Another good read-aloud by Lawson is *Rabbit Hill,* a Newberry Award winner in 1944.

L'Engle, Madeline. *A Wrinkle in Time.* Yearling, 1973.

Fantasy with a solid foundation of Christian principles woven into its fabric best describes the work of Madeline L'Engle. In the triumph of good over evil, Meg Murry and her younger brother Charles rescue their father from the great brain in the kingdom of Comazotz. Sequels are *The Wind in the Door* and *A Swiftly Tilting Planet.*

Lenski, Lois. *Strawberry Girl.* Lippincott-Raven, 1989.

Your children will miss out on this classic Newberry Medal book (a memorable part of my own childhood) if you don't read it aloud. Lenski specialized in writing regional books for children, descriptions of real-life families in diverse locations of the United States. This story of the Florida Crackers tells the story of ten-year-old Birdie Boyer, whose family grows strawberries. The idiomatic speech, customs, and superstitions may seem strange to your child, but when read aloud with feeling, this story will come alive.

Lewis, C. S. *The Lion, the Witch, and the Wardrobe.* HarperCollins Juvenile, 1994.

If you have limited time for reading aloud, let the *Chronicles of Narnia* be your very first choice. This seven-book series was written by an Oxford professor who had no children of his own but clearly understood the strong need of children for fantasy and magic. The Narnia series can be enjoyed on two levels—as a marvelously told tale of adventure and drama and as a Christian allegory that portrays the death and resurrection of Christ. The famous wardrobe that inspired these stories can be viewed at Wheaton College (Illinois), where many of Lewis's papers and letters have been collected. Here are the other titles: *Prince Caspian, The Silver Chair, The Magician's Nephew, The Horse and His Boy, Voyage of the Dawn Treader,* and *The Last Battle.*

Lindgren, Astrid. *Pippi Longstocking.* Viking Childrens, 1997.

The irrepressible Pippi Longstocking will shock and delight your children with her antics. Her mother has died and her father was lost at sea. Consequently she lives alone, a fact that intrigues her two young next-door neighbors. Other Pippi titles are *Pippi Goes on Board* and *Pippi in the South Seas.*

Lowry, Lois. *Number the Stars.* Houghton Mifflin, 1989.

Winner of the 1990 Newberry Medal plus multiple other awards, this is a wonderful portrayal of youthful courage. A ten-year-old Danish girl and her family take in a Jewish friend whose life is threatened by the Nazis in 1943. You may need to supply some historical background as you're reading, but this book is an ideal way to introduce your child to the historical reality of the Holocaust. Lowry is a prolific author whose *Anastasia Krupnik* series has long been a favorite of middle-grade readers. Lowry has a marvelous gift of characterization and writes with humor and realism.

McCloskey, Robert. *Homer Price.* Viking, 1976.

Homer Price is the quintessential small-town boy and Centerburg is his town. Homer's most famous escapade involves a doughnut machine gone berserk. Looking for a diamond bracelet that slipped into the batter provides all the incentive people need to buy up Homer's inventory of doughnuts. *Centerburg Tales* relates more of Homer's all-American antics.

Macdonald, George. *The Princess and the Goblin.* Illustrated by Arthur Hughes. Puffin, 1997.

George Macdonald, the famed nineteenth-century Scottish storyteller, was revered by later writers of fantasy such as C. S. Lewis, J. R. R. Tolkien, and Charles Williams. Heroism blends with clear images of good and evil in a narrative of rescue that fascinates from beginning to end. You will thrill as the little princess is rescued from the mountain goblins by Curdie. Also by the author: *The Christmas Stories of George Macdonald.*

MacLachlan, Patricia. *Sarah, Plain and Tall.* Harper Trophy, 1987.

A moving story, beautifully told. I am deeply touched whenever I read this tale of a widower farmer with two children who advertises for a wife. Sarah, plain and tall, arrives and although she misses the Maine seashore, she soon becomes mother to Caleb and Anna and wife to Papa.

Mains, David and Karen. *Tales of the Kingdom.* Illustrated by Jack Stockman. David C. Cook, 1983.

This book was made for reading aloud. Hero, the orphan boy; Princess Amanda; and Dirty, the pig girl, are the characters in this moving, beautifully illustrated Christian parable. Enjoy this volume and its sequels, *Tales of the Resistance* and *Tales of the Restoration,* in front of the fireplace after dinner.

Montgomery, Lucy Maud. *Anne of Green Gables.* Simon and Schuster, 1994.

The first novel in this well-loved series, originally published in 1908, tells the story of Anne Shirley, an outspoken eleven-year-old orphan sent to live with an elderly couple who actually wanted a strong boy to help them out. If you continue the series, you can follow Anne through adolescence to motherhood of six children.

Norton, Mary. *The Borrowers.* Harcourt Brace, 1998.

This book has been going strong for almost fifty years. It has intrigued hundreds of thousands of children with its tale of little people who live beneath the floorboards of an English country house. Children are fascinated with the way the Clock family borrows things from "human beans" to make their home livable (for example, a pocket watch for a clock, a doll's tea set for dishes, and matchboxes for a chest of drawers). When little things are missing in your household, you'll no doubt blame it on the "borrowers" after you've read this book.

O'Dell, Scott. *The Hawk That Dare Not Hunt by Day.* Bob Jones University Press, 1975.

This historical novel recreates the life and times of William Tyndale (the hawk that dare not hunt by day), whose mission was to put a Bible in the hands of every common man. The story is told by a fictional smuggler who distributes Tyndale's Bible in London. You'll learn a great deal about European life in the sixteenth century while marveling at Tyndale's vision and courage.

O'Dell, Scott. *Island of the Blue Dolphins.* Houghton Mifflin, 1960.

This title won a Newberry Award in 1960 and was subsequently made into a film. A twelve-year-old Indian girl tries to save wild dogs that remain on the island from which her tribe has been removed. Her pluck and courage are inspiring to middle graders.

Paterson, Katherine. *Bridge to Terabithia.* Harper Trophy, 1987.

A Newberry Award winner, this story tells of the relationship between a ten-year-old boy in rural Virginia and a newcomer to his town. Leslie, the newcomer, and Jess become fast friends and are inseparable until the tragedy of her death when she tries to reach Terabithia, their hideaway, during a storm.

Peck, Robert Newton. *Soup.* Yearling, 1979.

There has never been a pair of friends as likeable as Rob Peck and his best friend, Soup. We know that Soup, otherwise known as Luther Wesley Vinson, went on to become a minister, but when he and Rob Peck were growing up in a rural Vermont town in the 1920s, there was little mischief they didn't make. These books are surefire winners for engaging reluctant readers. Other titles are *Soup and Me, Soup for President, Soup on Wheels, Soup's Drum,* and *Soup's Goat.*

Raskin, Ellen. *The Westing Game.* Puffin, 1992.

This Newberry Medal–winning mystery is one you can solve together as a family. Award your own prize to the first child who can come up with the solution.

Rawls, Wilson. *Where the Red Fern Grows.* Starfire, 1984.

The emotional impact of this story about a boy and his two dogs is a strong one. If you live with a child who has begged for a dog of his own or who deeply loves the dog he has, this story is must reading. Although it is often listed as a young adult book, I have found that mature middle-grade students enjoy it and benefit from the excellent writing. There is also an audiocassette available.

Robinson, Barbara. *The Best Christmas Pageant Ever.* Harpercrest, 1987.

If you've ever been in, directed, or watched a Sunday school Christmas program, this hilarious story will definitely be a favorite in your family. Imagine your Christmas program being taken over by a boorish bunch of kids who smoke cigars, talk dirty, and have absolutely no respect for anybody. Their total lack of understanding about the real meaning of the Christmas story only adds to the confusion. Make this a yearly read aloud tradition at your house. You'll be reminded in a humorous and offbeat way of what the holiday is really all about. Also look for *The Best School Year Ever.*

Selden, George. *Cricket in Times Square.* Illustrated by Garth Williams. Farrar, Straus and Giroux, 1963.

This is the wonderful story of Chester Cricket, who was transported in a picnic basket from Connecticut to Times Square, New York. All of the characters in this read-aloud are memorable: Harry the Cat, Tucker the Mouse, and of course Mario Bellini, the little boy who befriends and cares for Chester. I read this story to the first fifth-grade class I taught and have reread it dozens of times, always with great success. A sequel is *Tucker's Country-side*.

Speare, Elizabeth George. *The Bronze Bow.* Houghton Mifflin, 1997.

This Newberry Medal book is set in Galilee during the time of Jesus and tells the story of a young Jewish rebel and his attraction to Jesus and his teachings. The characterizations are vivid and the action is exciting. This book will make an impact on your entire family. Some families have used it as a springboard for discussing the similarities between Palestine in Jesus' time and Israel today.

Taylor, Sydney. *All-of-a-Kind Family.* Yearling, 1980.

A peek into an engaging turn-of-the-century New York Jewish household. In an age of vanishing values and disappearing dinner table conversations, this book provides a heartwarming and happy story. Girls will identify with at least one of the five sisters, and only children will yearn even more desperately for siblings.

Thomasma, Kenneth. *Soun Tetoken.* Illustrated by Eunice Hundley. Baker, 1992.

This historically accurate portrayal of a Nez Perce Indian boy in the late 1800s is part of the *Amazing Indian Children* series. These well-researched stories make great read-alouds, especially if you're traveling through one of the many settings that Thomasma has chosen for his stories. Other titles include *Kunu: Winnebago Boy Escapes; Pathki Nana: Kootenai Girl Solves a Mystery; Naya Nuki: Shoshoni Girl Who Ran; Amee-nah: Zuni Boy Runs the Race of*

His Life; Moho Wat: Sheepeater Boy Attempts a Rescue; and *Om-kas-toe: Blackfeet Twin Captures an Elkdog.*

Tolkien, J. R. R. *The Hobbit or There and Back Again.* Illustrated by Michael Hague. Houghton Mifflin, 1989.

There are many versions of this classic, but this recently published one is beautifully illustrated by Michael Hague and worth having. This is an ambitious read aloud project but one that will give you and your children of all ages much to think and talk about. If you enjoy fantasy with Christian allegory skillfully interwoven, this book is for you. Bilbo Baggins is our hero and along with the wizard Gandalf and his band of dwarves, he faces all manner of dangers and terrors. *The Fellowship of the Ring, The Two Towers,* and *The Return of the King* comprise *The Lord of the Rings* trilogy and continue the story of the hobbits. The trilogy is more suitable for reading aloud to older children.

Travers, P. L. *Mary Poppins.* Buccaneer, 1981.

Mary Poppins, the literary world's most famous nanny, flew in on an east wind one autumn evening and changed young Jane and Michael Banks's lives forever. Please don't watch the movie before you read the book.

Travis, L. *Redheaded Orphan.* Baker, 1995.

The *Ben and Zack* series includes three books about a pair of resourceful twelve-year-old boys—one black and one white—whose friendship is set during the Civil War. In this adventure Ben moves to Minnesota, where his father's outspoken stance against racial prejudice stirs up a community that is hostile toward local Indians. There's a lot of great history and some important lessons about friendship and loyalty in these read-alouds. Other books in the series are *Captured by a Spy, Thief from Five Points,* and *Union Army Black.*

White, E. B. *Charlotte's Web.* HarperCollins, 1952.

> This was one of our family's favorite read-alouds. White is such a fine writer that his story can be savored like fine chocolate. Adults will enjoy this tale as much or more than children will. Charlotte is a gray spider who plans with Fern, the farmer's daughter, to save the life of Wilbur the pig. He is to be slaughtered, and the animals of the barnyard look to Charlotte to save him. She spins messages in her web proclaiming Wilbur's worth. Be prepared to shed tears at the conclusion of this story. White's other offerings for children are *Stuart Little* and *The Trumpet of the Swan.*

Wilder, Laura Ingalls. *Little House in the Big Woods.* Illustrated by Garth Williams. Harper, 1971.

> The eight books in this series are a fictional account of the author's life in the late nineteenth century. Set in Wisconsin and on the plains of South Dakota, the stories abound with pioneer adventures that kids love. Parents will appreciate the strong faith and inspiring courage of the Ingalls family. The remaining books in the series are *Little House on the Prairie, Farmer Boy, On the Banks of Plum Creek, By the Shores of Silver Lake, The Long Winter, Little Town on the Prairie,* and *These Happy Golden Years.*

Yates, Elizabeth. *Amos Fortune, Free Man.* Puffin, 1989.

> This Newberry Honor Book tells the story of Amos Fortune, an African prince who was sold into slavery in 1725. Brought to America and sold at auction, he worked as a slave in Massachusetts until he bought his freedom at the age of sixty. Fortune's story is an inspiring tale of how to find true freedom and happiness.

Poetry

The volumes of poetry recommended to you in chapters 3 and 4 will continue to be suitable for reading aloud at this age level. These additional volumes are especially selected for the eight to twelve age group.

Kennedy, X. J., editor. *Knock at a Star.* Little, Brown, 1985.

> In addition to being an excellent volume of poetry, this title is a teaching tool. Through small collections of poetry the editor lets us know what poems do: make you laugh, tell stories, send messages, share feelings, and start you wondering. Other major sections include "What's Inside a Poem," "Special Kinds of Poetry," and "Do It Yourself." This book is mandatory for the budding poetry writer.

Prelutsky, Jack. *The New Kid on the Block.* Illustrated by James Stevenson. Green-willow, 1984.

> I prefer Prelutsky to Silverstein any day. His poems have wonderful humor and are eminently readable.

Silverstein, Shel. *Where the Sidewalk Ends: The Poems and Drawings of Shel Silverstein.* HarperCollins Juvenile, 1974.

> Silverstein's wacky sense of humor and uninhibited observations on the world will delight even the most reluctant poetry reader. Kids are always checking this one out of the library. If irreverence offends you, however, choose another poet. Also by Silverstein: *The Light in the Attic* and *The Giving Tree.*

Classics

Classics are stories that have withstood the test of time. They're still in print, often in dozens of different editions. They have been retold, revised, reissued, and revisited hundreds of times. Your children should be exposed to all or at least some of them as part of becoming literate adults. Reading the classics aloud is one way to bring alive the rich language and more complex plots that today's children (used to reading dumbed-down versions and comic book adaptations) find difficult to handle. Our family has the following recommended classic titles on our own bookshelves; they were favorites in both my husband's and my childhoods. Since all of the recommendations have been published in a variety of editions, only authors and titles (along with their original dates of publication) are listed. Find them in libraries, bookstores, used book stores, garage sales, and even free on the Internet (see resource D for Web sites that contain the complete texts of classics).

Alcott, Louisa May

Little Women, 1868. This classic (which has recently been popularized by the film) chronicles the life of the four March sisters in nineteenth-century New England. You'll fall in love with domestic Meg, artistic Amy, gentle Beth, and my personal favorite and heroine, tomboyish Jo.

Little Men, 1871. The second book in the March family series follows sister Jo and her husband, Professor Bhaer, who run a school in the country for boys, both rich and poor, that is remarkable for its atmosphere of love and learning.

Jo's Boys, 1886. This is the final book in the series about the March family in which Jo's students have grown up and are making their way in the world.

Eight Cousins or the Aunt-Hill, 1875. Orphaned Rose Campbell has to cope with six aunts and seven rambunctious boy cousins when she comes to live at the Aunt Hill.

Rose in Bloom, 1876. A sequel to *Eight Cousins.* Rose has grown up and after traveling in Europe returns to America to discover that she is loved more for her money than herself.

An Old-Fashioned Girl, 1870. Readers love the characters in this portrayal of American life in the nineteenth century. Polly makes friends with a wealthy Boston family and in the process learns the truth about the true relationship of happiness and riches.

Carroll, Lewis

Alice in Wonderland, 1865. *Through the Looking Glass and What Alice Found There,* 1871. For the child who loves fantasy and wacky humor, there are plenty of both in these classics, often sold as one book. Everyone needs to meet Alice, the Mad Hatter, the White Rabbit, and the Cheshire Cat. Look for the edition illustrated by Michael Hague for a lovely gift (Holt, Rinehart, Winston, 1985).

Defoe, Daniel

The Life and Adventures of Robinson Crusoe, 1719. The story of Englishman Robinson Crusoe, who lasted for thirty years on the desert island where he was shipwrecked, will whet your appetite for more "survival in the wilderness" stories (try *My Side of the Mountain* and *The Swiss Family Robinson*).

Dickens, Charles

A Christmas Carol, 1843. A must for reading during the Christmas holidays. There are dozens of versions of this title, but one you might want to consider for purchase contains Dickens's own performance text, cut and adapted by him for reading aloud in ninety minutes. The book is beautifully illustrated in watercolor and colored pencils by Carter Goodrich (William Morrow, 1996).

Dodge, Mary Mapes

Hans Brinker or the Silver Skates, 1915. If you live in a climate where ice skating is de rigueur, you'll enjoy this story. As part of my Dutch heritage, I'm very partial to it. A brother and sister learn lessons of sharing and sacrifice as they compete for first prize, the silver skates, in an annual skating race over the frozen canals of Holland.

Sewell, Anna

Black Beauty, 1877. Horse lovers will delight in this story of a fine nineteenth-century English horse and his life with a variety of masters. The characters are real, the descriptions are vivid, and the emotions will rise and fall as Black Beauty experiences life with a cruel London cab driver before being reunited with his beloved young first mistress. You may need to explain some settings and vocabulary in the story to make it come alive for your children.

Spyri, Johanna

Heidi, 1880. Please don't be put off by the advanced vocabulary in the original edition and succumb to reading an abridged edition or some bland retelling of this classic. Only the original will do. Heidi's life is a two-part adventure: life on an Alpine mountain with her stern grandfather and the goats; and life in the big city as a companion to Clara, a wealthy little girl who cannot walk. This book was one of my childhood favorites.

Stevenson, Robert Louis

Treasure Island, 1881–1882. A treasure map leads to a pirate fortune as well as adventure, excitement, and danger.

Kidnapped, 1886. Don't just think of this as a book for boys. After a young man is sold into slavery, he is saved in a shipwreck. It's slow going at the beginning and the Scottish Highlander dialect might prove a bit troublesome, but keep reading and you'll be rewarded with tales of bravery and friendship.

Twain, Mark

The Adventures of Tom Sawyer, 1876. Tom Sawyer is one of those resourceful and mischievous literary characters who should not be missed in the original.

The Adventures of Huckleberry Finn, 1884. A poor white boy, Huck Finn, and a runaway slave, Big Jim, become friends while encountering all manner of adventures on a Mississippi River raft.

The Prince and the Pauper, 1882. A destitute child and Edward, Prince of Wales, have a chance encounter and end up exchanging lives and identities with one another.

Wyss, Johann David

The Swiss Family Robinson, 1814. A Swiss couple and their four children are shipwrecked on a deserted island and creatively make a new life for themselves.

Anthologies of Children's Literature

An anthology is a collection of stories that is handy to have available for read aloud sessions, particularly during a rainy day on vacation or an automobile trip. A collection gives you a variety of different selections all in one convenient and portable location.

Low, Alice, compiler. *The Family Read-Aloud Christmas Treasury.* Illustrated by Marc Tolon Brown. Little, Brown, 1995.

Everything you need to make your Christmas memorable can be found in this treasury: poems, songs, carols, and all of the favorite Christmas stories. Give it to your family this holiday season.

Paterson, Katherine, compiler. *Angels and Other Strangers: Family Christmas Stories.* HarperCollins, 1979.

A collection of stories that Katherine Paterson's husband, a Presbyterian minister, reads aloud each Christmas to their congregation. Paterson is the Newberry Medal–winning author of *Bridge to Terabithia* and *Jacob Have I Loved.* These stories will remind your family of the true essence of Christmas.

Russell, William F., compiler. *Classics to Read Aloud to Your Children.* Crown, 1992.

Russell has collected the most popular short stories, poems, legends, and myths into one handy volume. Look for Shakespeare, Mark Twain, Dickens, O. Henry, Jack London, Aesop, Washington Irving, and many others. If your classics education was neglected, pick up this handy book and bring it up to speed while you read aloud to your children. Also look for *More Classics to Read Aloud to Your Children.*

Trelease, Jim, compiler. *Hey! Listen to This: Stories to Read Aloud.* Penguin, 1992.

Trelease did everyone a huge favor when he compiled this book. He brings dozens of excerpts from well-loved books together in one place, extending and enriching them with background material about the authors and what they have written. I highly recommend this book for every family's read aloud shelf.

Legends, Myths, Folk and Fairy Tales

There are hundreds of wonderful retellings of individual folk and fairy tales complete with illustrations that are perfect for reading aloud to younger children (see chapter 4). However, if you wish to pursue folk and fairy tales in more depth, you will need complete anthologies. Here are some of the best.

Alderson, Brian, translator. *The Brothers Grimm: Popular Folk Tales.* Illustrated by Michael Foreman. Trafalgar Square, 1997.

This is a good collection of the more well-known Grimm tales as well as some lesser-known titles.

Hamilton, Virginia, compiler. *The People Could Fly: American Black Folktales.* Illustrated by Leo and Diane Dillon. Random Library, 1987.

The retelling of twenty-four African American folktales. There's a little bit of everything here: animal tales, fanciful and cautionary tales, and slave tales of freedom. Every child should be exposed to this aspect of our country's history.

Harris, Joel Chandler. *The Complete Tales of Uncle Remus.* Illustrated by Richard Chase. Houghton Mifflin, 1955.

The tales of Brer Rabbit, Brer Fox, Brer B'ar, and Brer Wolf are told by Uncle Remus, whose phonetic spelling of black dialect may take some practice before you get good. But take your time, explain along the way, and before long you'll be having a rollicking good time.

King, William, compiler. *Hans Christian Andersen's Fairy Tales: The Classic Children's Treasury.* Courage Books, 1996.

Eight Andersen fairy tales are each illustrated by a different artist. Among the stories included are "Silly Hans," "The Ugly Duckling," "Thumbelina," and my personal favorite, "The Princess and the Pea." These timeless tales teach many wonderful lessons; they should be part of every child's literary heritage.

Opie, Iona Archibald, compiler. *The Classic Fairy Tales.* Illustrated by Peter Opie. Oxford University Press, 1983.

The Opies are the "first family" of nursery rhymes and fairy tales, experts to be sure. Here they have collected twenty-four well-known fairy tales as they were first presented in English. This is a book for the purist and collector.

Osborne, Mary Pope, compiler. *American Tall Tales.* Illustrated by Michael McCurdy. A. A. Knopf, 1991.

Meet Paul Bunyan, Pecos Bill, John Henry, Davy Crockett, Storm Along, and other larger-than-life characters from our country's rich heritage of folklore.

Owens, Lily, compiler. *The Complete Brothers Grimm Fairy Tales.* Grammercy, 1993.

Perhaps you've enjoyed "Cinderella" and "Rapunzel" with little appreciation for the brothers Grimm who authored them, along with more than two hundred additional tales.

Owens, Lily, compiler. *The Complete Hans Christian Andersen Fairy Tales.* Grammercy, 1993.

Owens has collected more than 150 of Andersen's fairy tales, among them "The Ugly Duckling," "The Emperor's New Clothes," and "Snow Queen."

Phelps, Ethel Johnston. *The Maid of the North.* Henry Holt, 1987.

This is a unique collection of twenty-one folk and fairy tales from around the world that depict women as bright, brave, crafty, determined, loving, and moral.

Singer, Isaac Bashevis. *Stories for Children.* Sunburst, 1991.

These are traditional Jewish folktales told with humor and realism. My students loved to hear "Zlateh the Goat" and "The Fools of Chelm."

CHAPTER Six

Books to Entice the Reluctant Reader

• • •

Literature is my Utopia. Here I am not disenfranchised. No barrier of the senses shuts me out from the sweet, gracious discourse of my book friends. They talk to me without embarrassment or awkwardness.

Helen Keller

As a school librarian, I was often faced with the task of helping Stuart find a book. Stuart was a reluctant reader. He would wander through the library stacks with his hands in his pockets trying to look busy. But the astute observer could tell that Stuart was simply not interested in choosing a book to read on his own. The trick to helping children like Stuart find books was to suggest a title that was on their independent reading level with a story line that was intriguing enough to catch and hold their interest. Once they finished that book, one had to have several more like it ready to thrust into their hands.

A book for a reluctant reader needs to be easy to read, have a predictable plot, and feature characters to whom children can easily relate. I often sold children like Stuart on the idea of reading by introducing them to Encyclopedia Brown, a young detective. Readers try to outsmart the author and have a chance to check on their sleuthing powers by comparing their solution to the author's. Once a reluctant reader like Stuart had read one Encyclopedia Brown adventure, he could hardly wait to begin the next.

Do you remember the first time you fell for a series of books? Maybe it was *Nancy Drew* or the *Sugar Creek Gang*. They certainly don't qualify as great literature, but these books meet a need that many children have for repetition and predictability. The recommendations in this chapter will not necessarily stand the read aloud test, but they will usually entice a reluctant reader who is uneasy with complicated plots, difficult vocabulary, and unusual characters and settings. Of course, the recommendations in this chapter aren't just for reluctant readers. Avid readers will enjoy these stories also!

The books in this category are most appropriate for children between the ages of eight and twelve, although there is leeway on either end of the age guidelines depending on interest and reading ability.

Bibee, John. *Home School Detectives.* InterVarsity Press, 1994–98.

> As a result of solving a thirty-year-old robbery in their hometown of Springdale, three boys and their sisters become known as the Home School Detectives. Their adventures aren't limited to Springdale, however, as the following titles demonstrate: *The Mystery of the Mexican Graveyard, The Mystery in Lost Canyon,* and *The Mystery at Broken Bridge.*

Buchanan, Paul, and Rod Randall. *The Misadventures of Willie Plummet.* Concordia, 1998–99.

> Thirteen-year-old Willie has some amazing adventures and you can go along for the ride. Titles like *Invasion*

from Planet X, Ballistic Bugs, and *Gold Flakes for Breakfast* are sure to entice a reluctant reader.

Cleary, Beverly. *Ramona* books and *Henry* books. Dell.

Although this author was included in the read aloud section, both of these series are attractive to a child who wants characters that remind her of people she knows. Once children discover the humor and real-life situations, they'll want to read nonstop through all of them: *Ramona and Her Father; Ramona the Brave; Ramona Quimby, Age Eight; Ramona Forever; Ramona the Pest;* and *Beezus and Ramona.* Another very popular Cleary series (especially for boys) revolves around an engaging young man named Henry. Titles are *Henry Huggins, Henry and Ribsy, Henry and the Paper Route, Henry and the Clubhouse,* and *Henry and Beezus.*

Hutchens, Paul. *Sugar Creek Gang* series. Moody.

This enduring adventure series that combines Christian values and wholesome stories is over fifty years old and still going strong. I loved it when I was growing up and saved my allowance to buy as many titles as I could. Some of my favorites then and now include *The Killer Bear, The Winter Rescue, The Lost Campers,* and *The Secret Hideout.* If you have the money and time, you can purchase and read over thirty *Sugar Creek Gang* books.

Jackson, Dave and Netta. *Trailblazer* books. Bethany, 1997–98.

The *Trailblazer* books are thrilling adventure stories that introduce young readers to Christian heroes of the past. Titles include *Defeat of the Ghost Riders,* featuring Mary McLeod Bethune; *The Fate of the Yellow Woodbee,* about missionary hero Nate Saint; and *Spy for the Night Riders,* the story of Martin Luther. There are more than two dozen titles.

Janney, Rebecca Price. *The Impossible Dreamers.* Multonomah, 1997–98.

This time-travel series is piloted by Thomas Jefferson Wakesnoris, whose three home-schooled students are the beneficiaries of his predisposition to fall asleep at any time or place, but especially in the middle of history lessons. If he's concentrating especially hard he takes his young charges along with him to another time and place for field trips that are nothing like the ones you and I remember from our school days. Titles include *The Mystery of Loch Ness, Search for Amelia Earhart,* and *Secret of the Lost Colony.*

Johnson, Lois Walfrid. *The Riverboat Adventures.* Bethany, 1995–98, and *Adventures of the North Woods.* Bethany, 1990–98.

Johnson writes well-researched and exciting historical fiction. *The Riverboat Adventures* follow Libby, whose father is the captain of a Mississippi River steamboat. *Adventures of the North Woods* tells the story of Kate O'Connell, an early twentieth-century twelve year old who moves with her mom and stepdad to northwest Wisconsin.

Katz, Fred E. *Spine Chillers.* Tommy Nelson, 1996–98.

Does the world need another horror series? Only you can answer that question. This is, however, a less gruesome and more wholesome alternative to the popular *Goosebumps* series by E. L. Stine.

Leppard, Lois Gladys. *A Mandie Book.* Bethany, 1985–98.

This series relates stories about Mandie, a turn-of-the-century preteen in North Carolina. Titles are *Mandie and the Secret Tunnel, Mandie and the Cherokee Legend, Mandie and the Ghost Bandits, Mandie and the Forbidden Attic, Mandie and the Trunk's Secret, Mandie and the Medicine Man,* and *Mandie and the Charleston Phantom.*

Levene, Nancy Simpson. *Alex* series. Chariot Victor, 1989–96.

Easy reading devoted to typical preteen adventures. There are more than a dozen titles, each with a food theme, such as *Peach Pit Popularity, Mint Cookie Miracles,* and *The Salty Scarecrow Solution.*

Murphy, Elspeth Campbell. *The Three Cousins Detective Club.* Bethany, 1995–98.

Three ten-year-old cousins, Timothy, Titus, and Sarah, solve mysteries while learning proverbs from the Bible.

Myers, Bill. *Bloodhounds, Inc.* Bethany, 1998.

A new mystery series from the co-creator of *McGee and Me.* There are two titles so far with more to come: *The Ghosts of KRZY* and *The Mystery of the Invisible Knight.*

Myers, Bill. *McGee and Me* series. Tyndale.

Based on the video series developed by Focus on the Family, the book series features Nick and his cartoon creation, McGee. Each story teaches a lesson in life, with plenty of humor.

Packard, Edward. *Choose Your Own Adventures.* Bantam, 1982–98, and *Choose Your Own Nightmare.* Bantam, 1995–98.

The books in this series are never read straight through—a concept that really appeals to kids. Instead, the reader makes choices based on how she thinks the story will unfold. For example, if you decide it would be wiser to stay hidden in the cave, you turn to page 4. If you're adventuresome and want to set out through the tunnel, you turn to page 7. If the adventures are too calm, you can step up the excitement and choose nightmares by the same author.

Richardson, Arleta. *Grandma's Attic* series. Chariot Victor, 1994–98.

Nostalgia for times when Grandma (possibly Great-grandma) was a girl will entice your reluctant reader into this series. Titles are *Magical Memories, Pieces of Magic, Treasures from Grandma, Sixteen and Away from Home,* and *Eighteen and on Her Own.*

Robertson, Keith. *Henry Reed* series. Illustrated by Robert McCloskey. Viking, 1989–98.

The *Henry Reed* series isn't as easy to read or contemporary as some of the other series but the stories are extremely interesting. Henry gets older as the series progresses but in the beginning stories he is thirteen. He is one of the most likeable young men in children's literature. His various business enterprises, while profitable for him, can be hazardous to the health of the adults who are involved. Titles are *Henry Reed, Inc.; Henry Reed's Baby-Sitting Service; Henry Reed's Big Show; Henry Reed's Journey;* and *Henry Reed's Think Tank.*

Roddy, Lee. *D. J. Dillon* series. Chariot Victor, 1987–96.

Here are lots of exciting animal adventures set in the Sierra Nevada mountains by the creator of the TV show *Grizzly Adams.* Titles are *D. J. Dillon and the City Bear's Adventures; D. J. Dillon and Dooger, the Grasshopper Hound; D. J. Dillon and the Ghost Dog of Stoney Ridge;* and *D. J. Dillon and the Hair-Pulling Bear Dog.*

Sobol, Donald J. *Encyclopedia Brown* series. Illustrated by Leonard Shortall. Skylark, 1982–98.

Readers can work at solving the mysteries along with boy detective Encyclopedia Brown. Solutions for each ten- to twelve-page mystery can be found in the back of the book. Each volume contains ten mysteries. Some of the many titles are *Encyclopedia Brown Keeps the Peace; Encyclopedia Brown Gets His Man; Encyclopedia Brown Finds the Clues; Encyclopedia Brown and the Case of the Secret Pitch;* and *Encyclopedia Brown, Boy Detective.*

Stahl, Hilda. *Elizabeth Gail* series. Tyndale, 1989–98.

Elizabeth Gail Dobbs is a foster child, and this series tells about how she grows up and copes with the loss of her family. There are eighteen books in the series. Among them are *Elizabeth Gail and the Mystery at the Johnson Farm, E. G. and the Secret Box, E. G. and the Teddy Bear Mystery,* and *E. G. and the Dangerous Double.*

Warner, Gertrude Chandler. *Boxcar Children.* Albert Whitman, 1987–99.

I read my first Warner mystery in third or fourth grade and then proceeded to read the entire series. I'm still a mystery fan almost fifty years later. Your child will enjoy all of these titles: *The Boxcar Children, Surprise Island, The Yellow House Mystery, Mystery Ranch, Mike's Mystery, Blue Bay Mystery, The Woodshed Mystery, The Lighthouse Mystery, Mountain Top Mystery, Schoolhouse Mystery, Caboose Mystery, Houseboat Mystery, Snowbound Mystery, Tree House Mystery, Bicycle Mystery, Mystery in the Sand, Mystery Behind the Wall,* and *Bus Station Mystery.*

CHAPTER Seven

Rate Your School's Reading Quotient

• • •

Children are wired for sound, but print is an optional accessory that must be painstakingly bolted on.

Steven Pinker

I met the most challenging reluctant reader of my educational career when I took a job as a librarian in a suburban elementary school. As one of my first projects I campaigned for the adoption of a practice called Sustained Silent Reading (SSR). Some schools call it DER (Drop Everything and Read). In the Sustained Silent Reading program students read silently in class each day for a prescribed length of time. Their teachers join them.

"How can children," I questioned my fellow faculty members, "gain fluency and ease in their reading, if they don't practice?" The research was clear, then and now, about the importance of reading a lot if children are to become proficient readers. Our students weren't spending enough time curled up with good books and our reading scores reflected it.

"And further," I suggested, "how can children learn the value of reading and know the excitement of being transported to other times and places if they don't have adult role models?" Children are convinced more by what adults do than what they say.

All but one teacher was enthusiastic. She was dubious about the value of spending her valuable time reading in the classroom. "I don't like to read," she protested. "Why can't I grade papers instead?"

"You've totally missed the point," I told her, trying to keep my rising impatience under control. "You have to demonstrate to your students that reading is such a worthwhile activity that you'll even postpone grading papers or making lesson plans to do it yourself."

"Okay," she agreed. "But what will I read? I don't like to read." I wanted to fire her on the spot but I had no such authority. Instead, I thought about all of the reluctant readers I had tempted over the years with *Charlie and the Chocolate Factory* or *Charlotte's Web*. Clearly I would have to come up with something just a bit different for this well-past-middle-aged reluctant reader. I suggested a historical romance.

Before I knew it SSR was going full steam in her classroom. Whenever I peeked in her classroom during her scheduled period, every head was bent over a book, including hers. I could almost have predicted what happened next. Mrs. Armstrong wasn't just reading during SSR. She was reading during her lunch break in the teachers' lounge and while her students were in gym class. When she was nearly finished with the more than three-hundred-page book, she lamented its completion. "I need another one just like it," she said. I was ready for her.

My story has two points. First, it's never too late to get hooked on books. But second and more important, children need to have role models who demonstrate on a daily basis that reading is enjoyable and important. Teachers, principals, and other school personnel need to recognize the importance of reading and then develop and implement outstanding reading programs.

When I became an elementary school principal, I continued to motivate students and teachers with reading incentives, Battle of the Books programs,[1] daily read-alouds by teachers, and regular periods of silent reading in every classroom. Encouraging students to read a lot, however, is only one of the things that every school should be doing to help parents raise readers.

As a parent, you have every reason to expect that the school your child attends will teach your child to read, will emphasize the importance of reading, will provide many opportunities for your child to practice his reading skills, and will offer extra help to students who may be having problems. Perhaps you are uneasy about your child's reading progress or have questions about whether your school is doing a good job. How can you evaluate these things?

To begin, you can determine your school's reading quotient. Do this by finding answers to the questions in the reading quotient quiz that follows and then awarding points to your school based on your answers. Once you have computed your school's reading quotient, you'll be ready to examine your child's reading performance; chapter 8 will provide the information and resources you need. Knowing how well your child and his school are doing will help you make important decisions about schooling options or the need for a new approach to reading instruction.

To determine your school's reading quotient, answer the following questions.

1. Does your school or district or state have a set of organized reading standards indicating what students are supposed to master at each grade level? Teachers need to know what students are expected to learn and then

be held accountable for teaching it. Compare the standards to which your child is being held to the Reading/Language Arts Curriculum Framework for California, found on the Internet at http://www.cde.ca.gov/cilbranch/eltdiv/csmc.htm or the Texas Alternative Document at http://www.htcomp.net/tad. The California standards were developed in response to the failure of whole-language instruction programs in the state and are based on the most recent reading instruction research. The Texas Alternative Document was prepared by a group of Texas educators in response to what they believed to be a weak and watered-down state board of education proposal. It is also excellent.

If your school or district administration is holding students and teachers at every grade level accountable to a set of standards comparable to those in either of the two documents cited, give your school 5 points.

2. Are students tested periodically to determine if they are meeting the established standards? Formative tests (those given at intervals throughout the school year) are most helpful to teachers because they can then make immediate instructional changes (speed up, slow down, use a new approach, regroup). Summative tests (standardized state and/or national assessments) show how a child, school, or district compares to a larger testing sample but they are of no help in fixing the reading problems of individual students. All types of testing are essential.

If your school gives frequent formative reading tests throughout the school year, add 5 points. If your school gives a yearly standardized test (like the Iowa Test of Basic Skills or Metropolitan Achievement Test), add 5 points. If your school gives a yearly state assessment at required grade levels, add 5 points.

3. Is there a specific reading curriculum (basal reading series) that provides manuals for teachers and materials for students that are consistent in philosophy with the best practices in reading instruction as demonstrated by research, including phonemic awareness; structured, explicit phonics; a wide variety of decodable texts for student practice;[2] comprehension strategies; and use of well-written materials?

    If your school uses a specific reading curriculum as described above, add 5 points. If the curriculum does not meet the described criteria, subtract 10 points.

4. Are the teachers in your school trained to teach phonemic awareness; systematic, explicit phonics; and comprehension strategies? Do they do so regularly and with effectiveness? The research shows that many teachers are poorly trained to teach reading, particularly to those students with reading difficulties.[3] Determining the skill and expertise of teachers is a difficult task, even for administrators and supervisors. Advanced degrees and years of experience may be a partial indicator of a good teacher, but not always. Results (does every child learn to read?) are more credible indicators.

    If the teachers in your school are skilled in teaching reading as described above, add 5 points.

5. Does the principal speak knowledgeably about the school's reading instruction program? Does the principal have a stated reading improvement plan? Does a systematic process exist to remediate reading problems? Is the principal's philosophy of reading instruction consistent with the best practices recommended by the current research? Does he or she visit reading classrooms frequently and listen to children read regularly? If your child has a reading problem, is the principal aware of it? One of the key contributors to the quality of a school

is its principal. Read *The Principal's Guide to Raising Reading Achievement*[4] for a complete discussion of the principal's role in creating a school of readers.

If the principal of your school has made it possible for all children to learn to read, give 10 points. If the principal won't discuss reading with parents or recommends classroom practices that are not research-based, subtract 10 points.

6. Does your school teach research-based phonemic awareness and give explicit, systematic phonics instruction for all students in kindergarten and first grade? Here are the essential teachings that must take place for every child to learn how to read.[5]

• Teachers must begin teaching phonemic awareness (the conscious understanding that a spoken word is made up of a sequence of speech sounds) directly and explicitly at an early age, such as in kindergarten. Children must be trained to hear the individual sounds (phonemes) of their language. They must be able to disconnect, or "unglue," sounds in words in order to use an alphabetic writing system.[6] For example, they must be able to separate and hear each of the three sounds in the word *cat*. Educators and parents cannot count on all or even most children developing this awareness naturally; they must be taught. This skill is an absolutely essential prerequisite for learning to read and spell.[7]

The lack of phonemic awareness is the most powerful determinant of the likelihood of failure to learn to read. If children cannot hear and manipulate the sounds in spoken words, they will have an extremely difficult time learning how to map the sounds of our language to letters and letter patterns—the essence of decoding.[8] Phonemic awareness instruction should begin before instruction in sound-spelling relationships (phonics) and be continued throughout the teaching of sound-spelling relationships. See resource B for a complete list of phonemic awareness programs and student assessment materials.

• Teachers must teach each of the sound-spelling correspondences (phonics) explicitly and systematically. It is not enough to teach phonics in the context of a story (as whole-language proponents do) by introducing an isolated example and then expecting a child to figure it out on his own the next time he encounters the letter in print. This important aspect of reading instruction cannot be left to chance. The phonemes must be separated from the words for instruction. This can happen only if the teacher isolates each phoneme (sound) and then matches it up with the correct letter.

Be warned that most traditional phonics programs use the reverse logic: they begin with the letters (spelling) and then associate them with their corresponding sounds. This is very confusing to the beginning reader and even to many teachers. I specifically recommend the Lindamood and Phono-Graphix methods (see resource G for information) for their clarity and ease of instruction. These programs start by teaching the "one-to-one correspondences" (one sound to one letter), and when these are mastered, move on to "one-to-many correspondences" (one sound to several letters) and then to the "code overlaps" (those letters that have several different phonemes or sounds).

• Teachers must show children exactly how to sound out —decode—words through blending the individual sounds together. They must be shown how to move sequentially from left to right through spellings of words as they sound out, or say the sound for each spelling. Daily practice sessions should include the blending of only the sound-spelling relationships the children have learned to that point. This skill must be "overlearned" so that it becomes highly accurate and automatic. (See resource G for a complete list of recommended phonics programs).

• Teachers should provide an ample supply of code-based readers—books in which almost all of the words with the exception of high-frequency sight words can be sounded out by students—rather than ordinary literature during early instruction. For their own early independent reading experiences, using reading material that has too many words that children cannot decode independently encourages guessing, which may actually hinder reading development. Children need connected, decodable text to practice the sound-spelling correspondences they have learned. The integration of phonics and reading can only occur with the use of decodable text. Children can begin reading decodable text relatively quickly, since learning just a few sound-spelling correspondences will enable the reading of dozens of words. See resource H for a list of books that repeat phonetic elements in their stories.

• Teachers should correct oral reading errors. Whole-language instruction discourages teachers from correcting students who make errors, but children benefit when they receive corrective feedback.

• Teachers should read aloud interesting stories, picture books, poetry, and literature of all kinds to develop knowledge and comprehension. Teacher- and parent-read stories play a critical role in building children's oral language comprehension, which ultimately affects their reading comprehension. Story-based activities should be structured to build comprehension and vocabulary skills and should not include decoding skills. Teachers should read aloud to students several times during the school day and use these opportunities for discussion about text organization (fiction, nonfiction, poetry), vocabulary development, and general knowledge building.

• Teachers should use good literature to teach comprehension and use phonics to teach decoding but should not mix the two. A common misconception held by many educators is that if they are teaching sound-spelling relationships in the context of real stories (implicit instruction), they are teaching phonics. This is not the case. Mixing decoding and comprehension instruction in the same activity is less effective, even when the decoding instruction is fairly structured. When phonics instruction is embedded (implicit), it does not have the same instructional effect as when it is taught purely and separately and then practiced to mastery in decodable text.[9]

If your school offers a phonemic awareness program in kindergarten, add 10 points. If your school offers an explicit, systematic phonics program that is not embedded in whole-language instruction and gives students ample opportunity to practice their skills in decodable text, add 10 points. If your school does not have these two programs, subtract 10 points for each one it does not have.

7. Are the materials (readers, library books, etc.) that students are expected to read on a challenging instructional reading level? I'm aware of a subtle shift downward in the difficulty of reading materials for students. For example, one fifth grader I know recently listened

to *Beezus and Ramona* as an in-class read-aloud. I consider this book a suitable read-aloud for first and second grade; competent second- and third-grade readers should be able to read this book independently. Read-alouds ought to stretch and challenge students. With the growing trend toward allowing students to read anything as long as they're reading, they are more often choosing books that, while admittedly entertaining, offer little academic challenge.

If your school challenges students to read at or slightly above their independent level (see the definitions of independent, instructional, and frustration reading levels in chapter 8), add 5 points.

8. Does the school's reading program at every grade level emphasize the real purpose of reading: comprehension? Are students taught comprehension strategies and then given ample practice in content areas to perfect the strategies? If you are unclear about what comprehension strategies are or what they can do to help children become successful readers, consult *Improving Reading: A Handbook of Strategies*[10] or *Solving School Problems.*[11]

   If your school teaches comprehension strategies across the grade levels, add 10 points. If your school does not have a well-structured comprehension strategy instruction program, subtract 10 points.

9. Does each classroom have a variety of materials available for students to read during free time? Can students access books, newspapers, and magazines in every classroom?

   If your school encourages students to read by having materials available in every classroom, give 5 points.

10. Is there a library or resource center to provide a rich and varied sampling of library books for recreational reading? Reading instruction should never be limited

just to reading the "reading book." Students should be encouraged and/or required to read all kinds of books (biographies, poetry, science, fantasy, science fiction, etc.). Students who are reading short books without chapters should be permitted to visit the library every day or as often as needed to check out books for either independent reading or home read-alouds. Every student should be required to have a library book available for independent reading either at home in the evening or on his desk at school during the day. Every child needs a sturdy backpack to keep reading material moving back and forth between home and school. Teachers should monitor each student's independent reading.

If your school has a well-stocked media center staffed by a librarian (plus aides and volunteers) who encourages students to read, add 5 points. If all teachers monitor students' independent reading using charts, reading logs, book reports, etc., add 5 points. Subtract 5 points if either is missing.

11. Does your school offer meaningful remedial programs for those students who are having problems with phonemic awareness, phonics, or comprehension? The school that offers phonemic awareness instruction in kindergarten; systematic, explicit phonics instruction in first grade; and a steady dose of comprehension strategies at every grade level every day will have very few children who even need a remedial program. But some children will need an immediate adjustment of instruction to a small group or more intensive one-to-one teaching of phonemic awareness and phonics to pick up the skills they need. Others will need extra help in comprehension. Are there enrichment and accelerated programs for students who are superior readers?

If your school offers excellent remedial programs, add 5 points. If your school offers reading enrichment and acceleration, add 5 points. If your school waits until third grade to refer children for special help, or offers a watered-down program that does not systematically teach phonemic awareness or phonics, subtract 10 points.

12. Does your school welcome parents (and others) as volunteers in its classrooms and library? The effective school utilizes parent resources to work with students who may be having problems.

    If your school has an active volunteer program that supports reading instruction in the classrooms and library, add 5 points.

13. Does your school offer schoolwide reading incentive programs to motivate students to do more independent reading? Does the library have a book club or discussion group? Are there contests that give prizes for independent reading? Is there a schoolwide Sustained Silent Reading Program? Is there an opportunity for teams of middle-grade students to read books and answer questions like the Battle of the Books contests mentioned earlier? Beginning readers should read at least three to six short books of decodable text daily. Primary readers should read two to three longer books of decodable text or one to three chapters from a longer book daily. Middle-grade students need to read at least thirty-five to forty-five books per year to learn the vocabulary and concepts they need to become literate adults.

    For every program that encourages students to read, give 5 points.

Now, add up the points you've awarded your school to determine its reading quotient.

A+   100 or more points: superior reading quotient
A   90–100 points: excellent reading quotient
B   80–90 points: good reading quotient
C   70–80 points: poor reading quotient

If your school scored below 80 points I would recommend removing your child from it. The school needs a major reorganization and it will take longer than your child can wait to fix the problems. If your school has major areas of strength but needs improvement, find out what you can do to help. Do your homework and get involved. Chapter 9 offers suggestions about how you can work to improve reading instruction in your school.

CHAPTER Eight

Helping Your Child Learn to Read at Home and School

• • •

One of the most heartbreaking sights in American schools today is that of children—once so eager to read—discovering that they are not learning how. There comes over those sparkling eyes a glaze of listless despair. We are not talking about a few children and scattered schools. We are talking about millions of children and every school in the nation. And the toll in young spirits is the least of it. The toll in the learning and thinking potential of our citizenry is beyond measure.

Sylvia Farnham-Diggory

Saul, an energetic first grader, had been in three different schools during the year. He entered our school just as the year was coming to a close. Saul didn't know his alphabet, couldn't associate any sounds with their corresponding letters, and was restless and inattentive during reading class.

His teacher, Mrs. Karr, felt Saul would greatly benefit by repeating first grade. His father was devastated. "I flunked second grade," he said, with tears in his eyes. "I want better for my little boy. Just let me teach him over the summer. I know I can catch him up if you'll give me the chance."

Of course we gave him a chance, but we didn't just leave it up to him. We got Saul into a summer school program, arranged for a private tutor, and gave Saul's father a crash course in reading aloud every night. It was a busy summer for Saul's family, but they made some giant strides. When fall arrived, Saul wasn't a star reader yet, but he was well on his way, thanks to hard work and cooperation from everyone, including Saul.

Every student and parent deserves the chance to learn to read. And every teacher and principal should have the belief that all students can learn. If your child has experienced failure and discouragement along the way, she can be helped. However, as I told Saul's father, your efforts will take time, patience, understanding, and some professional assistance. With each passing school year of failure and defeat, the layers of discouragement and lack of self-worth make the job more difficult.

Does My Child Have a Reading Problem?

Perhaps you identify with Saul's father and have even endured similar parent-teacher conferences. Perhaps your child is a problem reader. Is she in the "low" reading group? Does she score more than a year or more below grade level on the standardized tests that are given in school? Does she have difficulty reading and understanding science and history assignments? Does she groan with dread when the teacher assigns a book report? If you answered yes to any of the above questions, you are probably living with a problem reader.

The list of achievements that should take place in the years from kindergarten through third grade (the point by which all children should be reading without difficulty) is a long one—it will no doubt surprise you when you turn to resource F, where it has been reproduced. The list, according to those who assembled it, is neither exhaustive nor incontestable, but it does capture how much a child must accomplish in four years to be a fluent and successful reader by the end of third grade. Your child's teacher should be able to tell you how your child is doing (or has done) on each of these items, and if you have been involved in your child's schooling, you will be aware of your child's progress in many areas.

There are dozens of standardized assessments that educational specialists in schools or tutoring centers can administer to children. Those options may not be practical or possible for you. To be referred to a school psychologist or learning disability specialist in the school setting, your child will have to be failing. This may not be the case. You may just suspect that she is capable of doing much better or that the school is unaware of her problem because they do not administer regular formative tests. So you may waste valuable time trying to convince school personnel to test your child. Even if you do get a testing referral approved, it can take so long, an entire school year can be wasted.

If you take your child to a tutoring center you will be charged, sometimes quite a lot, for the testing. I recommend testing your own child informally using three different methods: (1) to assess reading ability, use the Reading Competency Test developed by Dr. Patrick Groff and available from The National Right to Read Foundation;[1] (2) to assess reading ability and actual problems, do an informal test using your child's school text materials; and (3) to assess actual problems, use tests of phonological skills found in a book you should purchase.[2]

Assess Your Child's Reading Ability

The Reading Competency Test will help you determine your child's independent, instructional, and frustration reading grade levels. If these terms are unfamiliar to you, here is what they mean:

- The independent reading level is the highest level at which a child can read easily and fluently without assistance, with few errors in word recognition, and with good comprehension and recall.
- The instructional level is the highest level at which the child can do satisfactory reading, provided that she receives preparation and supervision from a teacher; errors in word recognition are not frequent, and comprehension and recall are satisfactory.
- The frustration level is the level at which a child's reading skills break down; fluency disappears, errors in word recognition are numerous, comprehension is faulty, recall is sketchy, and signs of emotional tension and discomfort become evident.[3]

The second way to assess your child's reading ability is to conduct an informal reading inventory with your child. Is your child's problem one of decoding (sounding out words)? Does she lack fluency and speed when she reads because she is stumbling over the words she can't sound out? Is she guessing at too many unknown words and consequently having a difficult time with comprehension? Can she decode with total accuracy but has difficulty in understanding and remembering what she has read? The informal reading inventory can help you find out.

If your child attends school and has a basal reading text, get permission from the teacher to use the text for three evenings. Explain that you want to hear your child read aloud. If your child is older, use a science, social studies, or literature textbook. Please be aware that many of today's textbooks are dumbed down, however, and so materials that would have been appropriate for a fourth or fifth grader to read are now being recommended for sixth or seventh graders. This dumb-ing-down process can make it more difficult for you to determine just how well or poorly your child is reading.

During these read aloud sessions, you should avoid pressuring or blaming your child. You are simply gathering information that will help you make decisions about how best to improve your child's reading ability. Simply follow these steps:

1. Set aside three twenty-to-thirty-minute blocks of time to read with your child.
2. Choose a story or selection that she has not yet read and discussed in school.
3. Have your child read the selection aloud.
4. Keep track of errors in pronunciation and omission of words and phrases. Five or more errors in a one-hundred-word sample indicate there may be decoding problems in her reading.
5. Ask your child ten questions about the story to test comprehension. Ask some factual questions: How many apples did Sally buy? Where did she buy them? Ask some inference questions: Why do you think Sally bought ten apples? Ask some sequence questions: Where did Sally go first after school? Where did she go next? If your child answers eight out of ten correctly, her comprehension is good. If she answers fewer than eight correctly, particularly if the questions were factual, the passage is too difficult for her.
6. Note your child's reading rate. Does she read at a conversational rate, somewhat slowly, or very slowly?

As a result of the reading sample, you should have some idea of where your child's reading problems lie:

- Decoding: ability to decipher and pronounce new words.
- Vocabulary: ability to figure out the meaning of new words.

- Factual comprehension: ability to answer questions about what has happened in the story.
- Inferential comprehension: ability to read between the lines and draw conclusions about the story.
- Sequencing comprehension: ability to place events in their proper sequence in the story.
- Reading rate: ability to read at an appropriate rate so that fluency and readability are maintained.

Regardless of your child's IQ or ability level, if she cannot decode, she will be unable to read well enough to comprehend. If your child is unable to complete any parts of the informal inventory using her textbooks, simply stop the test. You will learn more valuable information from the next set of assessments. Do not conclude that because your child is unable to read her textbooks that she has a disability or will be unable to learn to read. She simply needs to be taught using the right way.

The third method of assessment is actually a group of very short but excellent tests that can be found in the book *Reading Reflex*.[4] These tests assess blending, phoneme segmentation, auditory processing, and code knowledge skills. Many older children who do not read well have problems because of low phonemic awareness skills. Once most children learn these skills, they will be on their way to reading success.

Why Does My Child Have a Reading Problem?

Figuring out why your child is having a reading problem is somewhat like solving a mystery. You will need to be a clever detective to see if any of these reading restrictors is having a negative impact on your child's learning.

Health

Children must be able both to see and hear to learn to read. Deficiencies, even minor ones, in either area may severely impact reading ability. In ruling out possible causes of learning problems, always start here. Have your child's hearing and vision tested by physicians who are specialists. Most school systems offer vision and hearing screenings, but these screenings often do not catch or pay enough attention to marginal problems that can make it difficult for your child to learn to read.

Other health problems such as severe allergies or infections that cause a child to miss a great deal of school can impact learning. Regular attendance is very important, especially during instruction in beginning reading. Many children who do poorly in school have simply missed large chunks of instruction and do not have a good foundation on which to base new learning. Had they been regular attenders, their problems would be far fewer.

School

How can school be a reading restrictor? Unfortunately, in the hands of a poor teacher, even the most dedicated student can have learning problems. Talk with your child regularly about what is happening at school. Look over her homework, go to all scheduled parent conferences, and become an educated consumer of your school system, whether it is private or public. Determine your school's reading quotient (see chapter 7). Consult chapter 9 for ways to help improve your school's reading program. Sometimes your child's reading problem can be easily solved by transferring her to another school, another teacher, or by home schooling your child using one of the recommended programs found in resources B and G.

Moves

Children who move frequently may miss out on important skills. Make sure when you move that all records are transferred and that you are aware of the reading levels and abilities of your children. Monitor their placement, particularly in reading, as they enter a new school.

Home

Are there emotional factors in your family that cause your child to lie awake at night and worry? Is school attendance and achievement a low priority in your family? Or are you putting so much pressure on your child that she is responding with nervousness and failure? Do you neglect reading aloud with your children? Affixing blame is not nearly as important as solving the problem. However, if there are home patterns that should be changed, neglecting to address them will only cause the problem to grow worse.

Learning Ability

The child who appears to have average or above-average intelligence but still has problems learning to read may well have a learning disability, although there is a growing body of research to suggest that many problems formerly diagnosed as learning disabilities are actually teaching disabilities, use of the wrong methodology or not enough early, intensive one-to-one teaching. The learning-disabled child may have a short attention span, problems organizing herself and her homework, difficulty remembering spelling words, and problems controlling her behavior. Public schools are required by law to evaluate and offer services to children who have diagnosed learning disabilities. Find help.

Language Development

If your child was slow to develop speaking skills and even now has problems expressing herself, she may have speech and language problems that are inhibiting reading achievement. Children need lots of language input from adults to learn sentence structure, vocabulary, and grammar. This learning provides the base on which a child learns to read. See resource I for information about language development in children.

Social and Emotional Development

This last restrictor of reading achievement is most often seen in older children and adolescents. Problems that were evident in preschool and early elementary years may have gone unattended. Layers of failure and discouragement often result in poor attitudes or severe discipline problems that mask the reading problem. Most adolescents would rather be thought of as smart alecky or troublesome than dumb. Their feelings of self-defeat come out in antisocial ways, and failing to connect their behavior with the underlying academic problems, we leave the real problem untreated.

Teaching Your Child to Read at Home

Many parents I know have not been willing to trust their child's reading instruction to anyone else. With the advent of a total whole-language philosophy in many schools and classrooms, the chances of a child having reading problems have increased. If you want to be your child's first reading teacher or help your child become a better reader, I recommend a method that many parents are using with great success: Phono-Graphix (see resource G). This method teaches phonological processing (the ability to hear and manipulate sounds) and code knowledge (the ability to sound out words on the printed page). The method, which is contained in *Reading Reflex*,[5] can be used to teach very young children who have not yet had any formal instruction as well as older children who have been taught by other methods that haven't worked.

If your child's problem is strictly comprehension—she can decode any word she encounters but just can't answer questions or remember what she has read—you will need to take another route. Research has shown that adults and children with comprehension problems do not make mental pictures of what they read and consequently cannot remember well. The program I recommend for comprehension difficulties, produced by Lindamood-Bell, is called Visualizing and Verbalizing for Language Comprehension and Thinking. This program develops the brain's ability to visualize gestalts (wholes) by integrating imagery and language, using specific vocabulary to develop and describe components of mental representation. This is a program that you can do one-on-one with your child. It is one of three Lindamood products that are exceptional in both their quality and in the results they achieve (see resources B and G). Lindamood also operates clinics around the country for the treatment of very severe reading problems in children, adolescents, or adults.[6] If a loved one of mine had what seemed like an untreatable reading difficulty I'd run (not walk) to the nearest Lindamood clinic.

If you do not feel confident that you can teach your child yourself, hire a tutor to do the job. For many other recommended research-based phonics programs and reading methodologies, see resource G.

CHAPTER Nine

Seventy-Plus Ways to Raise a Reader

• • •

The more elements of good parenting, good teaching, and good schooling children experience, the greater the likelihood that they will achieve their potential as readers.

National Academy of Education
Commission on Reading

Reading is a complex skill that is related to the other communication skills: speaking, listening, and writing. The moment you begin speaking to your newborn child you are developing skills he will need to be a successful reader. The more language you provide in your child's life, either written or spoken, the greater his reading potential. Any activities that involve listening (following directions, hearing a story told or read aloud); speaking (retelling a story that has been read aloud, making up a story about pictures, or answering questions about a story); or writing build reading skills. The connection to reading may not always seem obvious to you, but fill your child's life with language (printed and spoken) and you will raise a reader.

Here are some concrete suggestions by age group for raising a reader.

Raising a Reader: Birth through Age 3

1. Create a place in your home for reading. Both adults and children need special places to keep their books and to curl up and read. Respect this need and encourage your children to learn how to spend time independently with books as well as care for their own books.
2. Read books that ask questions; read books that teach direction, numbers, time, and opposites; and read books that teach words and ideas. Every book you read is a teaching opportunity.
3. Give your baby time to look at the pictures, which should be held about eight to ten inches from his face.
4. Obtain a public library card for your child and as soon as he is old enough begin taking him to library story hours. Many libraries offer pajama party story hours for working families.
5. Create a special family tradition by giving blank books or scrapbooks for birthday and Christmas gifts. Inscribe a special message in the front cover of the book and affix a bookplate that says "When I Was Five" (or whatever the age). During the year paste birthday cards, postcards, awards, or pictures in various places in the books that commemorate the year's happenings. As your children get older, they can write short descriptions to go with the momentos. By the time your child graduates from high school he will have three dozen special books filled with remembrances. Writing short descriptions helps comprehension and sequencing. Talking about the pictures and cards and why they were chosen builds comprehension and speaking skills.

6. Begin to build your child's own personal library collection by carefully buying favorite books. Buy some of the books I have recommended in this book as well as those recommended by other authors from the list in resource C.
7. If bedtime doesn't work, read at naptime or breakfast. Find the time of day that works best for you, your child, and your busy schedule.
8. Don't expect your child to sit absolutely still while you're reading aloud. Some children may need to move around and be active.
9. Talk to your children about your work and explain what you are doing and why. Never underestimate the ability of your child to soak up information and concepts about your work. As your children get older, begin to teach them how to do simple tasks in the kitchen and workshop. Following directions and sequencing events builds comprehension skills. Language development and vocabulary development take place during these kinds of activities.
10. Be sensitive to your children's interests and read books that capitalize on them (for example, farm animals, trucks, dinosaurs).
11. Talk, read, and sing constantly to infants. They learn from everything they see and hear. Consult resource I for a wonderful collection of books that will give you ideas about language development and conversation with your child.
12. Take your baby to the park, zoo, grocery store, and anywhere else you're going. Draw his attention to objects, signs, and people along the way.
13. Always make books a part of your baby's toy selection, even if he enjoys handling books more than being read to. As your child grows, point out pictures of objects and label them with their correct names. Eventually your child will be able to name the pictures also.

14. Read recipes aloud while you're cooking. For those favorites of your children, consider printing out the recipe in large type on your computer and laminating it so your child can have his own copy on which to follow along. Put several together in book form.

15. Encourage the books-'n'-bedtime habit. After we read our bedtime story, my children always had their own books to read. I found that early morning was also a favorite time for them to read alone. This reduced the wake-up calls for Mom and Dad.

16. Always take your emergency book bag with you whenever you head to your car, even if it's only for a short trip to the grocery store. You never know when a flat tire or a dead battery will leave you with time in which to calm restless children. Take a vacation book bag with you for longer trips. Don't leave home without your read-alouds.

17. Encourage associations between symbols and their meanings. As your toddlers mature they will begin to recognize familiar signs (stop, yield, no right turn) and shout with delight at logos for cereal or fast-food restaurants.

18. Help toddlers make the transition from baby talk to adult language by repeating their words and expressions correctly back to them. This interplay of language should never be done in the spirit of reprimand or correction. Do it matter-of-factly and with an upbeat attitude.

19. Consider a books-in-the-bathtub habit. I always read in the tub and my kids liked to do it too, so we kept plastic books with our tub toys so they could copy Mom.

20. Encourage toddlers to "read" their favorite picture books to themselves while you're nearby to give encouragement and help (only if asked). Don't correct your child if he makes mistakes in vocabulary or plot. The point is not accuracy at this point in his reading career, but hav-

ing a positive reading experience. There will be plenty of time for correcting when your child begins to master decoding skills.

21. If Grandma and Grandpa live far away, ask them to make a video or tape recording of themselves reading several of your child's favorite stories. Play the recordings to build the bonds and memories across the miles.

Raising a Reader: Ages 4–9

22. Introduce your child to cassettes and read along books they can use independently whenever they want to hear a story. Purchase an inexpensive cassette player your child can operate on his own.

23. After a field trip to the zoo or science museum, have your children draw pictures of something special they enjoyed. Then have them dictate two or three sentences about the picture and start a scrapbook of your trips that your children can "read." If you took photographs add them later.

24. Help your children seek their own solutions to problems. We are often tempted as parents to solve every problem and meet every need our children bring to us, but helping them figure out ways to solve their own problems can help even the youngest child gain confidence and expand his ability to be persistent and learn independently.

25. Give your child a chalkboard (either an easel or lapboard will work), chalk, and/or a magic slate. Encourage scribbling and writing "words."

26. Buy a set of magnetic letters for the refrigerator and spell out familiar words and names for your child. As your child gains proficiency in spelling and reading, leave short messages, such as "I love you" or "Good morning." Messages on Post-its work well also.

27. Make your very own alphabet book using family pictures, pictures from magazines and catalogs, and photographs you take of objects your child likes.
28. Teach your child the familiar alphabet song.
29. Label familiar objects around the house to help your child learn new words.
30. Teach your child lots of finger- and handplays using the books recommended in chapter 4.
31. Leave messages for your child in his lunchbox, in his underwear drawer, anywhere, or send them through the mail.
32. When your preschooler or early elementary child gains familiarity with a story, read it aloud and leave out key words for him to fill in.
33. Capitalize on the curious nature of your child's mind and heart regarding spiritual matters and use the read aloud time to help answer sensitive questions, such as Where is heaven? Why do people die? Can God see everything I do?
34. Use your child's developmental stages to teach appropriate lessons through reading, such as the need for sharing and being kind to others.
35. Play rhyme, rhythm, and sound games with your child. Look for objects in pictures or around the house that begin with a specific letter of the alphabet.
36. Allow your child to select some of his own books to check out at the public library. Don't discourage your child from choosing a book you've already read or even checked out the week before. Children like to hear favorites read over and over.
37. Make a jigsaw puzzle from the dust jacket of a book, a large photo, or a favorite poster. Laminate it on thin cardboard at the copy store and then cut it into odd shapes. Your child will enjoy homemade puzzles more than those you purchase in the store. You can even use

a picture of Grandma and Grandpa or cousins who live far away to make the puzzle.

38. Make a recipe taken from one of your child's favorite books. Try green eggs and ham for your first culinary triumph (*Green Eggs and Ham* by Dr. Seuss) or an angel food cake using the recipe in *High Rise Glorious Skittle Skat Roarious Sky Pie Angel Food Cake* by Nancy Willard. You can also check out simple recipe books and make snacks or lunches together.

39. Buy some puppets and encourage your children to create their own puppet shows for the family.

40. Provide writing materials and give your children an opportunity to create their own stories. They may have to explain them to you since the scribbles will frequently be unintelligible to an adult.

41. Capture every opportunity for reading as you take minitrips and run errands together. Point out street signs, grocery store displays, and other types of informational signs.

42. Get acquainted with the children's librarian at your public library. Help your children understand that this is a person who can help them find answers to questions they have or make suggestions for good books to read. Model asking the librarian to help you. If you don't know how to find books in the library using the card catalog or computer terminal, learn so that you can model this process for your children whenever you visit the library.

43. Find a good used bookstore and visit it often. Books don't have to be brand new to be enjoyed.

44. Tell stories in addition to reading them aloud. An old family album is the perfect catalyst for jogging tired memories.

45. Create a family bulletin board or place (magnets on the refrigerator work well) for projects and written work

to be displayed. As soon as your child begins to draw pictures and "write" stories, display his work.

Raising a Reader: Ages 10–12

46. Whenever you take a trip, make a scrapbook. Mount brochures, postcards, and placemats and help your children write a travelogue to accompany the memorabilia. The whole family will enjoy looking at the trip books (even more after the children are grown) to relive your family vacations.
47. Set aside time every day to read aloud together as a family. Read after dinner for fifteen to twenty minutes. Once you start the habit, you'll find it to be the highlight of the day.
48. Be open-minded and receptive to your children's ideas. Listen with interest to your children's questions, ideas, and suggestions. Your respect for your child's mind will be appreciated and become the basis for a lifelong closeness.
49. Help your child write a book review for one his favorite books and post it on amazon.com for the world to read. Make sure you proofread it together for grammar and spelling correctness.
50. Publish a family or neighborhood newsletter. This is an especially good project for the summertime.
51. Check out craft and/or how-to books and use the directions to make or build something.
52. Build model airplanes or model rockets. Following written and pictorial directions is a great reading experience.
53. Encourage your child to write thank-you notes for gifts received and special events to which he has been invited.
54. Require outside reading from your children even if their teachers don't. Turn off the TV and read. Set aside time

each day for your child to read on his own. This is a particularly important thing to do during summer vacations when children have more time and need to keep their reading skills up to speed.

55. Subscribe to a teenage (or even adult) magazine. Reluctant readers love to read about people who are slightly older than they are. There are also dozens of excellent special-interest magazines available. *Ranger Rick* and *National Geographic World* were both favorites of my children and children still devour them.

56. Play word games like Scrabble and Boggle with your children and introduce them to crossword puzzles.

57. Help your child write a letter to the editor of the newspaper about a controversial issue in the community.

58. Help your child find books about famous sports stars or contemporary heroes.

59. Find movies based on books. Watch them and then read the books. Try *The Black Stallion, Little Women, Call of the Wild, All Things Bright and Beautiful.*

Raising a Reader: Your School, Your Community, the Country

60. Organize a Battle of the Books program for the middle-grade students in your school: A reading list of about forty books is selected; questions are written for each book; students form teams and then compete by answering questions about the books. This contest is an excellent way to stimulate reading and encourage academic competition. For help in getting started use *Books, Battles, and Bees.*[1]

61. Invite speakers to PTA meetings that are knowledgeable about reading instruction.

62. Work to raise funds through the PTA to purchase books for the school library.

63. Organize a Birthday Book Program at your school, where parents purchase a book for the school library on their child's birthday.

64. Offer to organize a schoolwide reading incentive program. Run a reading lottery in which students fill out tickets for each hour of reading time. Deposit the winning tickets in a barrel and draw for prizes. Local merchants could donate them or you could award tickets to a baseball game.

65. Establish a paperback book exchange staffed by PTA members. Students turn in their old paperbacks and are given credits to select others in exchange.

66. Organize a course for parents through the local high school adult education program. The course could introduce parents to the process of how children learn to read and suggest ways for them to reinforce the school reading program at home.

67. Volunteer to coordinate the National Library Week or Children's Book Week with special programs in your school. One school made a large bulletin board with pictures and letters from all of the faculty members telling what books had made the most difference in their lives.

68. Find authors in your community who are willing to talk to students about writing; correspond with authors and publish their letters; or arrange a conference call with a famous author. Invite community leaders and business people to read their favorite stories aloud to classes.

69. Persuade a local business to award young readers with gift certificates to encourage recreational reading. Pizza Hut has had great success with its Book-It program, which awards certificates for pan pizzas when students complete goals they have set for themselves. You may want to involve a local business in your reading incen-

tive program to make it more relevant to your community. Get everyone involved.

70. Volunteer to help your child's teacher coordinate a special reading program. Use PTA or school funds to purchase read aloud tapes and books along with inexpensive tape recorders. Students can check out the tapes and books to take home.

71. Volunteer to form a parent-teacher task force to involve more parents in the community in the reading achievement of their students.

72. Organize a program in which faculty and administration report to parents on the academic performance of their students in the area of reading.

73. Lead a campaign to establish a library in your school if you don't already have one.

74. Run for the school board and become involved in policy-making decisions regarding curriculum. If you're really concerned about what is happening in your schools, there is no better place to have an impact.

Conclusion

● ● ●

"I would ask you to remember this one thing," said Badger. "The stories people tell have a way of taking care of them. If stories come to you, care for them. And learn to give them away when they are needed. Sometimes a person needs a story more than food to stay alive. That is why we put these stories in each other's memory. That is how people care for themselves."

Barry Lopez

"Raise a child in the way he should go . . ."

When I was the bone-weary mother of two preschoolers, I often felt like asking that whiny question often heard on extended car trips: "Are we there yet?" I wanted instant children without the daily grind. My experience with growing grass from seed actually resembled my parenting. I purchased the seed. I read the directions. I scattered the seed along with fertilizer and I began to water. The box said to keep the seed moist and was most emphatic about the importance of daily watering. On more than a few days, I didn't feel like watering. I couldn't see results. But I persevered; I was intimidated by the directions that threatened dire consequences if I was delinquent.

The day passed when the seed was supposed to have germinated; I continued to water. Just when I was beginning to think my efforts were for naught, I glimpsed a few green shoots. I was immediately more motivated to keep these baby blades of grass alive. Periodically I doubted the worth of my efforts. "It's never going to look like the picture on the box," I lamented. But each day a few more green shoots poked through the soil. At a distance I could see patches of pale green fuzz, a portent of things to come. My hard work was beginning to pay off. I couldn't neglect the watering, however. The new green shoots needed almost constant attention, it seemed. Warmer days demanded multiple waterings, and fertilizer was also recommended. I wanted to quit. I began to wish I'd ordered instant grass.

Those tender green shoots are like your child's reading ability. The printed word is the seed and your reading aloud is the watering. During much of the time you are reading aloud, you will never know what is being learned. But you must have faith that if you water (read) during the almost interminable germination period, the seed (your child's reading ability) will grow and flourish.

"Parents, respect your children . . ."

You're bone weary. The day has been filled with a number of minor irritants—a cranky child, a broken washing machine, and a misunderstanding with a coworker. When you finally get the kids ready for bed and look forward with longing to a few minutes of quiet before tackling some laundry, the children remind you with glee that you've forgotten their bedtime story.

You look forward to something short and snappy. The children want to hear *Bread and Jam for Frances.* "But," you protest, "we've read that one before." In fact you've read the book so often that your mouth ceases to water anymore at the delightful descriptions of the meals that Frances's mother fixes to tempt her away from bread and jam. Impatient and irritable, you raise your voice just above its normal tone and assert your parental rights. "We're not reading that book again. We've read it before!" You lose the argument and for very good reasons. Your children have already developed opinions and tastes about the books they enjoy; respect those opinions. The read aloud time belongs to your children.

When our first child was born after five years of being a two-career couple, my husband didn't turn into superdad overnight. He was a bit reluctant to become involved with the more mundane tasks of diapering and toilet training. Anytime I left home for more than an hour, he needed several pages of instructions. So when I drove away from home late one evening to the local hospital with severe abdominal pains, he was more than a little anxious about my leaving him with a spunky three year old and a just-learning-to-walk one year old. The fact that I took the only car along with me made him even more distraught.

"You'll be okay," I reassured him. "If they wake up, feed them and read them a story."

"What kind of story?" he quizzed me.

"They have their favorites. Just read the same one over and over again."

"But I'll go crazy," my husband responded.

"I know!" I smiled, knowingly. "But you'll be okay. I probably won't be gone long." I was at the hospital for a week. My nearly ruptured appendix was gangrenous.

This was the week that my husband became a real father. Not only did he discover how much real work is involved in parenting small children, but he also began to understand the comfort that hearing familiar stories over and over again brings to small children. But he still asked, "Why do they have to hear the same story so many times?"

I didn't have the time to explain to him then that children have an insatiable need to hear the same stories, poems, and rhymes read over and over again. I think we were interrupted by the diaper delivery man arriving with reinforcements.

Our adult brains can tolerate perhaps a dozen readings of *Green Eggs and Ham* before the plot becomes fairly predictable. Unless you understand the importance that repetition plays in the development of the child, you will be tempted to utter those words: "We've read that book before." But remember, each time you read the book aloud to your child, a new word may become part of her vocabulary, a new insight about a relationship or small detail of the story will become clear, or some part of an illustration will suddenly be noticed for the first time.

And then there is the sheer joy of hearing the language used in all of the wonderful ways that authors and poets have put it together. Do you tire of hearing the Twenty-third Psalm read aloud, particularly when you are in need of solace or comfort? Do you stand up in church on Sunday when a familiar hymn is sung once more to shout, "We've sung that one before!" Respect your child's need for repetition and familiarity in the read aloud process.

"Whatsoever things are true, whatsoever things are honest, think on these things . . ."

Boys and girls in the preschool and early elementary years soon begin to make more of their own choices from the shelves of the libraries you use. They will often bring books home from their school libraries for you to read aloud. They may sometimes choose books that aren't well written or have a point of view with which you disagree.

Make the most of the early years when your children are receptive to your opinions and judgments to begin subtly shaping their choices and explaining the reasons why certain books or stories are more worthy of their consideration. As children grow older and begin to read more independently, the area of choice can become a battleground. You may think that what your child is reading is not appropriate. You may feel your child is choosing material that is too easy or too repetitious. Often children get into reading ruts with series like *Nancy Drew, Hardy Boys,* or *Choose Your Own Adventure.* You may feel your children are wasting time.

I'm not certain how many Grace Livingston Hill novels I borrowed from the church library before I realized that I knew the stories better than Grace did. The point is, let your child make the choice. Let your child decide when she is tired of a particular style. Left to explore various styles and types of writing, the child will soon become bored and move on to other more challenging choices.

Have faith in your child's ability to choose and make judgments about what is well written and worthy based on the wide variety of excellent literature you've introduced to her over the years. Don't censor what your child reads. Do discuss with your child the reasons why you like or dislike certain authors, values or lifestyles, or types of writing. Then permit your child to make those judgments for herself based on the foundation you've laid. Early exposure to good writing and Christian ideals will allow your young person to make her own decisions wisely as she reaches maturity. The exciting part is seeing her make choices on her own that parallel the ones you would have made for her.

Raising readers brings lifelong rewards. Emily and Patrick still call or e-mail me to discuss what they're reading and writing. They give me books as gifts for my birthday and Christmas. I recommend my favorites to them. They send articles and clippings to me and read the books I've written. I read their doctoral research with my dictionary in hand, hoping to make sense of a new field of study. Reading and writing will always connect my children and me; the foundation was laid in the rocking chair. It all began with Noah's Ark and Mother Goose.

Reading List about Reading Instruction

• • •

Adams, Marilyn Jager. *Beginning to Read: Thinking and Learning about Print.* Cambridge, Mass.: MIT Press, 1990.

This well-written and eminently readable book summarizes many of the critical issues surrounding whole language and phonics as well as updating Jeanne Chall's *Learning to Read: The Great Debate.* Adams came down on the side of a balanced approach to reading instruction, which managed to offend just about everybody who wants his or her way to be first, best, and only.

Balmuth, Miriam. *The Roots of Phonics.* New York: McGraw-Hill, 1982.

This is a straightforward volume of history and scholarship. If you want to understand at what point in history we lost confidence in the alphabetic code and the roles that Horace Mann and John Dewey played in its demise, check this book out.

Chall, Jeanne. *Learning to Read: The Great Debate.* 2nd ed. New York: McGraw-Hill, 1983.

You will need to read this book as background if you want to understand all of the discussion and argument that has ensued.

Flesch, Rudolph. *Why Johnny Can't Read.* New York: Harper and Row, 1955.

____. *Why Johnny Still Can't Read: A New Look at the Scandal of Our Schools.* New York: Harper and Row, 1981.

Both of these books are somewhat inflammatory and may raise your blood pressure but they are instructive concerning some of the political issues involved in the debate. They will definitely cause you to think.

Hall, Susan L. and Louisa Cook Moats. *Straight Talk about Reading.* New York: Contemporary Books, 1998.

Honig, Bill. *Teaching Our Children to Read: The Role of Skills in a Comprehensive Reading Program.* Thousand Oaks, Calif.: Corwin, 1996.

Honig is on a mission to help educators remain research-based while combining the best of both worlds—"a comprehensive, organized skill development and a literature driven and language rich language arts program" (vii). This is a readable book and an excellent desk resource.

Juel, Connie. *Learning to Read and Write in One Elementary School.* New York: Springer-Verlag, 1994.

This well-written book is an outstanding ethnographic study describing what it takes to bring the children of the poor to reading competency. The author believes that first-grade reading comprehension is almost always a matter of word recognition.

McGuinness, Diane, *Why our Children Can't Read and What We Can Do About It: A Scientific Revolution in Reading.* New York: Free Press, 1997.

This book lives up to the promise of its title. You'll understand why so many students aren't learning to read and what you can do about it in your school and community.

Spalding, Romalda Bishop, and Walter T. Spalding. *The Writing Road to Reading.* New York: William Morrow, 1990.

If you don't really understand phonemic awareness and haven't a clue about what phonics really is, find this updated and revised classic from 1957 and read it. You'll be intrigued by what you find, I promise.

Stotsky, Sandra. *Losing Our Language: How Multicultural Classroom Instruction Is Undermining Our Children's Ability to Read, Write, and Reason.* New York: Free Press, 1999.

Stotsky is a Harvard professor who has extensively studied reading textbooks. You will be alarmed at the extent to which our children's reading materials are being used to promote a multicultural agenda while at the same time being dumbed-down.

Materials to Assess
and Teach Phonemic Awareness

• • •

Adams, Marilyn J., Barbara Foorman, Ingvar Lundberg, and Terri
    Beeler. *Phonemic Awareness in Young Children*. Baltimore: Brookes,
    1998. To order, call 800-638-3775.

Byrne, Brian, and Ruth Fielding-Bansley. *Sound Foundations*. Artar-
    mon, New South Wales, Australia: Leyden Educational Pub-
    lishers. To order, write the publisher at 36 Whiting Street, Artar-
    mon, New South Wales, Australia, or call 02-439-8755.

Catts, H., and T. Vartianen. *Sounds Abound*. East Moline, Ill.: Lin-
    guiSystems, 1993. To order, write the publisher at 3100 4th Ave.,
    East Moline, IL 61244 or call 800-776-4332.

Lindamood-Bell Human Learning Managment System. *The Lin-
    damood Phoneme Sequencing (LiPS) Program*. San Luis Obispo,

Calif.: Lindamood-Bell Human Learning Management System. To order, call 800-233-1819.

Lundberg, Frost, and Peterson. *The Lundberg Kindergarten Phoneme Awareness Curriculum.* Baltimore: Paul H. Brookes. To order, call 800-638-3775.

Notari-Syverson, Angela, Rollanda E. O'Connor, and Patricia Vadasy. *Ladders to Literacy: A Preschool Activity Book.* Baltimore: Paul H. Brookes. To order, call 800-638-3775.

O'Connor, Rollanda E., Angela Notari-Syverson, and Patricia F. Vadasy. *Ladders to Literacy: A Kindergarten Activity Book.* Baltimore: Paul H. Brookes. To order, call 800-638-3775.

Robertson, C., and W. Salter. *The Phonological Awareness Book* and *The Phonological Awareness Kit.* East Moline, Ill.: LinguiSystems, 1995. To order, write the publisher at 3100 4th Ave., East Moline, IL 61244 or call 800-776-4332.

Torgesen, J., and B. Bryant. *Phonological Awareness Training for Reading.* Austin, Tex.: Pro-Ed. To order, call 512-451-3246.

Resource C

Resources to Help You Choose the Best in Books for Your Children

• • •

Although all of the books included in the reading lists in chapters 3, 4, 5, and 6 were in print and available for purchase through amazon.com or your local bookstore, the titles listed below may not always be in print or readily available for purchase. They will, however, usually be available for checkout at your public library or they can be borrowed through interlibrary loan.

Allison, Christine. *Teach Your Children Well: A Parent's Guide to the Stories, Poems, Fables and Tales That Instill Traditional Values.* New York: Delacorte, 1993.

Association of Christian Schools International. *Survey of Recommended Reading Lists: Preschool through Grade Twelve.* Colorado Springs: Association of Christian Schools International, 1998. To order, write the publisher at PO Box 35097, Colorado Springs, CO 80935-3509.

Cascardi, Andrea E. *Good Books to Grow On: Guide to Building Your Child's Library from Birth to Age 5.* New York: Warner, 1985.

Children's Book Council. *Children's Books: Awards and Prizes.* New York: Children's Book Council, 1992.

Coles, Robert. *The Call of Stories: Teaching and the Moral Imagination.* Boston: Houghton Mifflin, 1989.

Copperman, Paul. *Taking Books to Heart: How to Develop a Love of Reading in Your Child.* Reading, Mass.: Addison-Wesley, 1986.

Cullinan, Bernice E. *Literature and the Child.* New York: Harcourt Brace Jovanovich, 1981.

Cullinan, Bernice E. *Read to Me: Raising Kids Who Love to Read.* New York: Scholastic, 1992. Practical ideas in an easy-reading style.

Family Research Council. *Home Remedies: Reading Lists and Curriculum Aids to Promote Your Child's Educational Well-Being.* Washington, D.C.: Family Research Council. Contains helpful references, readings lists, and curriculum aids. To order, call 800-225-4008.

Gallagher, Susan V., and Roger Lundin. *Literature through the Eyes of Faith.* New York: Harper and Row, 1989.

Gillespie, John, and Diana Lembo. *Introducing Books: A Guide for the Middle Grades.* New York: Bowker, 1970.

Glaspey, Terry. *Children of a Great God.* Eugene, Ore.: Harvest House, 1995.

Gross, Jacquelyn, with Leonard Gross. *Make Your Child a Lifelong Reader: A Parent-Guided Program for Children of All Ages Who Can't, Won't, or Haven't Yet Started to Read.* Los Angeles: Jeremy P. Tarcher, 1986.

Hunt, Gladys. *Honey for a Child's Heart: The Imaginative Use of Books in Family Life.* Grand Rapids: Zondervan, 1989.

———. *Reading for Your Life: Turning Teens into Readers.* Grand Rapids: Zondervan, 1992.

Kilpatrick, William, Gregory Wolfe, and Suzanne M. Wolfe. *Books That Build Character.* New York: Simon and Schuster/Touchstone, 1994.

Kimmel, Margaret Mary, and Elizabeth Segel. *For Reading Out Loud: A Guide to Sharing Books with Children.* New York: Delacorte, 1983.

Lamme, Linda, with Vivian Cox, Jane Matanzo, and Miken Olson. *Raising Readers: A Guide to Sharing Literature with Young Children.* New York: Walker, 1980.

Lindskoog, Kathryn, and Ranelda Husicker. *How to Grow a Young Reader.* Wheaton, Ill.: Harold Shaw, 1999.

McMullan, Kate Hall. *How to Choose Good Books for Kids.* Reading, Mass.: Addison-Wesley, 1984.

Nehmer, Nancy L. *A Parent's Guide to Christian Books for Children.* Wheaton, Ill.: Tyndale House, 1984.

O'Connor, Karen. *How to Hook Your Kids on Books: Create a Love for Reading That Will Last a Lifetime.* Nashville: Thomas Nelson, 1995.

Oppenheim, Joanne, Barbara Brenner, and Betty D. Boegehold. *Choosing Books for Kids: Choosing the Right Book for the Right Child at the Right Time.* New York: Ballantine, 1986.

Rudman, Masah Kabakow, Anna Markus Pearce, and the editors of Consumer Reports Books. *For Love of Reading: A Parent's Guide to Encouraging Young Readers from Infancy through Age 5.* Mount Vernon, N.Y.: Consumers Union, 1988.

Sabine, Gordon, and Patricia Sabine. *Books That Made a Difference.* Hamden, Conn.: Shoe String, 1983.

Trelease, Jim. *The Read-Aloud Handbook.* New York: Penguin, 1995.

White, Dorothy. *Books before Five.* Portsmouth, N.H.: Heinemann, 1984.

Williams, Jane A. *How to Stock a Home Library Inexpensively.* Placerville, Calif.: Bluestocking Press, 1995.

Wilson, Elizabeth. *Books Children Love: A Guide to the Best in Children's Literature.* Wheaton, Ill.: Crossway, 1987.

Wilson, George, and Joyce Moss. *Books for Children to Read Alone: A Guide for Parents and Librarians.* New York: Bowker, 1988.

Web Sites about Books and Reading

● ● ●

If the book lover in you needs to read about the Internet before you'll feel comfortable surfing, check out this book: *Researching on the Internet: The Complete Guide to Finding, Evaluating and Organizing Information Effectively* by Robin Rowland and Dave Kinnaman (Rocklin, Calif.: Prima, 1995). To order, call 916-632-4400.

While each of the listed sites was operable and provided the indicated information at time of publication, I apologize for any changes that may have occurred since then.

Amazon.com. Access at http://www.amazon.com

An incredible online source of books for purchase. Use it also as a resource tool to find books on specific topics, meet popular authors through online interviews, or send a personal book review of your favorite titles.

Arizona Parents for Traditional Education. Access at http://www.theriver.com/Public/tucson_parents_edu_forum/

Provides helpful links to a variety of reading research and illustrates what activist parents are doing on the Web to change the way reading is taught.

The Center for the Future of Teaching and Learning. Access at http://www.cftl.org/

Contains an excellent synthesis of research on reading instruction from the National Institute of Child Health and Human Development.

Christian Classics Ethereal Library. Access at http://ccel.wheaton.edu/

Contains "classic Christian books in electronic format, selected for your edification." From early church fathers to modern authors, this source includes classic theological and fictional works by Augustine, Dante, Calvin, Milton, Edwards, Dostoyevsky, and many others. Also contains major reference works, such as *Matthew Henry's Commentary, Nave's Topical Bible,* and *Vine's Expository Dictionary.*

Encyclopedia Britannica Online. Access at http://www.eb.com/

You can sign up for a seven-day free trial subscription and check current subscription rates at this site. In addition to the complete text of articles from *Encyclopedia Britannica,* the site also contains several special features.

The English Server. Access at http://english-www.hss.cmu.edu/

This site is managed by students, faculty, and staff at Carnegie Mellon University. Over 15,000 texts in many disciplines: philosophy, literature, history, language studies and theory, music and music theory, and much more.

ERIC. Access at http://www.indiana.edu/~eric_rec/ieo/bibs/phonics.html

This Web site has a wealth of research information, bibliographies, and special reports about phonics and its use in the classroom.

My Virtual Reference Desk. Access at http://www.refdesk.com

This site contains dictionaries, magazines, newspapers, a list of search engines, and more information than you'll ever have time to use. It will be a bit overwhelming in the beginning, so plan to spend some time getting acquainted.

The Internet Book Information Center. Access at http://sunsite.unc.edu/ibic/

A guide to books and book-related resources on the Internet. "The grand-daddy of book-related sites on the Internet," according to *Publishers Weekly.*

Internet Public Library. Access at http://www.ipl.org/

Contains an index of thousands of online books. A reference librarian is available. You can find the complete texts of over 7,500 books, among them many of the classics listed in chapter 5, such as *Treasure Island, The Adventures of Tom Sawyer, The Adventures of Huckleberry Finn,* and *The Prince and the Pauper.*

Kids Web: A World Wide Web Digital Library for Schoolkids. Access at http://www.npac.syr.edu:80/textbook/kidsweb/

If your kids love to hunt for information, introduce them to this site with links to all kinds of reference sources, such as *Bartlett's Familiar Quotations, Biographical Dictionary, World Factbook,* maps, and census information, plus sites on social studies, science, sports, and much more.

The Learning First Alliance. Access at http://www.readbygrade3.com/lfa.htm

Comprised of a variety of educational organizations
(e.g., National Association of Elementary School Principals, American Federation of Teachers, National PTA),
the alliance has developed an excellent position paper/
consensus statement on reading and reading instruction
that should be read by every educator and parent.

The National Right to Read Foundation. Access at http://www.jwor.com/nrrf.htm

The National Right to Read Foundation has as its
mission the return of phonics and good literature to
every school in the nation. There are a variety of
interesting links on this site as well as materials for
purchase.

Resources for Parents and Educators. Access at http://www.elainemcewan.com

This is my own personal Web site. It contains information and resources to help parents and educators
with the most challenging problems of schooling
and parenting plus links to many other interesting
sites.

**The Reading and Language Arts Curriculum Framework for California. Access at
http://www.cde.ca.gov/cilbranch/eltdiv/cdsmc.htm**

An outstanding document that other states could do
well to emulate. Along with the Texas Alternative
Document (see below), it provides a comprehensive
list of what children should learn during their entire
school careers in the subjects of reading, writing,
and speaking.

The Riggs Institute. Access at http://www.riggsinst.org

A nonprofit organization that promotes the teaching of
phonics.

The Texas Alternative Document. Access at http://www.htcomp.net/tad

A complete set of language arts (reading, writing, speaking) curriculum standards. If you want to make sure

that your children are learning what they should, then compare what they're learning to this set of standards. I hope you'll be pleasantly surprised!

Treasure Island: Children's Literature and Classics for Teens. Access at http://jol lyroger.com/treasureisland.html

Visit this site for the texts of *Anne of Green Gables, Huckleberry Finn, A Little Princess,* and many others.

Trivium Pursuit Home Page. Access at http://www.muscanet.com/~trivium/

Great links to a variety of literary and curricular sites.

Predictable Books

• • •

Predictable books can play an important part in developing print awareness, phonemic awareness, and prereading skills in young children. Before long your child will be "reading" with you and to you.

Although all of the books included in the reading lists in chapters 3, 4, 5, and 6 were in print and available for purchase through amazon.com or your local bookstore, the titles listed below may not always be available for purchase. They will usually, however, be available for checkout at your public library or they can be borrowed through interlibrary loan.

Books with Repetitive Language Patterns

Hutchins, Pat. *Good Night, Owl!* New York: Macmillan, 1972.
Keats, Ezra Jack. *Over in the Meadow.* New York: Four Winds, 1972.

Martin, Bill. *The Haunted House.* New York: Holt, Rinehart and Winston, 1970.

Peek, Merle. *Roll Over!* New York: Houghton Mifflin, 1981.

Presto, Edna M. *The Temper Tantrum Book.* New York: Viking, 1969.

Westcott, Nadine Bernard. *I Know an Old Lady Who Swallowed a Fly.* Boston: Little, Brown, 1980.

Books with Repeated or Cumulative Story Events

Carle, Eric. *Do You Want to Be My Friend?* New York: Croswell, 1971.

dePaola, Tomie. *Pancakes for Breakfast.* New York: Harcourt Brace Jovanovich, 1978.

Hutchins, Pat. *Rosie's Walk.* New York: Macmillan, 1968.

Books with Repetitive Language Patterns and Repeated or Cumulative Story Events

Carle, Eric. *The Very Hungry Caterpillar.* Cleveland: Collins-World, 1969.

Galdone, Paul. *Henny Penny.* New York: Houghton Mifflin, 1975.

Galdone, Paul. *The Three Billy Goats Gruff.* New York: Houghton Mifflin, 1973.

Tolstoi, Alexei. *The Great Big Enormous Turnip.* New York: Franklin Watts, 1968.

Zemach, Margot. *The Judge.* New York: Farrar, Straus and Giroux, 1969.

Accomplishments in Reading

• • •

There are certain accomplishments you should look for in your child as you evaluate her reading ability and your school's reading program. Use the following lists as guides.

Kindergarten Accomplishments

1. Knows the parts of a book and their functions.
2. Begins to track print when listening to a familiar text being read or when rereading own writing.
3. "Reads" familiar texts emergently, i.e., not necessarily verbatim from the print alone.
4. Recognizes and can name all uppercase and lowercase letters.
5. Understands that the sequence of letters in a written word represents the sequence of sounds (phonemes) in a spoken word (alphabetic principle).

6. Learns many, though not all, one-to-one letter-sound correspondences.
7. Recognizes some words by sight, including a few very common ones (a, the, I, my, you, is, are).
8. Uses new vocabulary and grammatical constructions in own speech.
9. Makes appropriate switches from oral to written language situations.
10. Notices when simple sentences fail to make sense.
11. Connects information and events in texts to life and life to text experiences.
12. Retells, reenacts, or dramatizes stories or parts of stories.
13. Listens attentively to books teacher reads to class.
14. Can name some book titles and authors.
15. Demonstrates familiarity with a number of types or genres of text (e.g., storybooks, expository texts, poems, newspapers, and everyday print such as signs, notices, labels).
16. Correctly answers questions about stories read aloud.
17. Makes predictions based on illustrations or portions of stories.
18. Demonstrates understanding that spoken words consist of a sequence of phonemes.
19. Given spoken sets like "dan, dan, den" can identify the first two as being the same and the third as different.
20. Given spoken sets like "dak, pat, zen" can identify the first two as sharing a same sound.
21. Given spoken segments can merge them into a meaningful target word.
22. Given a spoken word can produce another word that rhymes with it.
23. Independently writes many uppercase and lowercase letters.
24. Uses phonemic awareness and letter knowledge to spell independently (invented or creative spelling).

25. Writes (unconventionally) to express own meaning.
26. Builds a repertoire of some conventionally spelled words.
27. Shows awareness of distinction between "kid writing" and conventional orthography.
28. Writes own name (first and last) and the first names of some friends or classmates.
29. Can write most letters and some words when they are dictated.

First-Grade Accomplishments

1. Makes a transition from emergent to "real" reading.
2. Reads aloud with accuracy and comprehension any text that is appropriately designed for the first half of grade 1.
3. Accurately decodes orthographically regular one-syllable words and nonsense words (e.g., sit, zot), using print-sound mappings to sound out unknown words.
4. Uses letter-sound correspondence knowledge to sound out unknown words when reading text.
5. Recognizes common, irregularly spelled words by sight (have, said, where, two).
6. Has a reading vocabulary of 300 to 500 words, including both sight words and easily sounded out words.
7. Monitors own reading and self-corrects when an incorrectly identified word does not fit with cues provided by the letters in the word or the context surrounding the word.
8. Reads and comprehends both fiction and nonfiction that is appropriately designed for grade level.
9. Shows evidence of expanding language repertory, including increasing appropriate use of standard more formal language registers.
10. Creates own written texts for others to read.

11. Notices when difficulties are encountered in understanding text.
12. Reads and understands simple written instructions.
13. Predicts and justifies what will happen next in stories.
14. Discusses prior knowledge of topics in expository texts.
15. Discusses how, why, and what-if questions in sharing nonfiction texts.
16. Describes new information gained from texts in own words.
17. Distinguishes whether incomplete sentences are incomplete or fail to make sense; notices when simple texts fail to make sense.
18. Can answer simple written comprehension questions based on material read.
19. Can count the number of syllables in a word.
20. Can blend or segment the phonemes of most one-syllable words.
21. Spells correctly three- or four-letter short vowel words.
22. Composes fairly readable first drafts using appropriate parts of the writing process (some attention to planning, drafting, rereading for meaning, and some self-correction).
23. Uses invented spelling/phonics-based knowledge to spell independently, when necessary.
24. Shows spelling consciousness or sensitivity to conventional spelling.
25. Uses basic punctuation and capitalization.
26. Produces a variety of types of compositions (e.g., stories, descriptions, journal entries), showing appropriate relationships between printed text, illustrations, and other graphics.
27. Engages in a variety of literary activities voluntarily (e.g., choosing books and stories to read, writing a note to a friend).

Second-Grade Accomplishments

1. Reads and comprehends both fiction and nonfiction that is appropriately designed for grade level.
2. Accurately decodes orthographically regular multisyllable words and nonsense words (e.g., capital, Kalamazoo).
3. Uses knowledge of print-sound mappings to sound out unknown words.
4. Accurately reads many irregularly spelled words and such spelling patterns as diphthongs, special vowel spellings, and common word endings.
5. Shows evidence of expanding language repertory, including increasing use of more formal language registers.
6. Reads voluntarily for interest and own purpose.
7. Rereads sentences when meaning is not clear.
8. Interprets information from diagrams, charts, and graphs.
9. Recalls facts and details of texts.
10. Reads nonfiction materials for answers to specific questions or for specific purposes.
11. Takes part in creative responses to texts such as dramatizations, oral presentations, fantasy, play, etc.
12. Discusses similarities in characters and events across stories.
13. Connects and compares information across nonfiction selection.
14. Poses possible answers to how, why, and what-if questions.
15. Correctly spells previously studied words and spelling patterns in own writing.
16. Represents the complete sound of a word when spelling independently.
17. Shows sensitivity to using formal language patterns in place of oral language patterns at appropriate spots in

own writing (e.g., decontextualizing sentences, conventions for quoted speech, literary language forms, proper verb forms).

18. Makes reasonable judgments about what to include in written products.
19. Productively discusses ways to clarify and refine writing of own and others.
20. With assistance, adds use of conferencing, revision, and editing processes to clarify and refine own writing to the steps of the expected parts of the writing process.
21. Given organizational help, writes informative, well-structured reports.
22. Attends to spelling, mechanics, and presentation for final products.
23. Produces a variety of types of compositions (e.g., stories, reports, correspondence).

Third-Grade Accomplishments

1. Reads aloud with fluency and comprehension any text that is appropriately designed for grade level.
2. Uses letter-sound correspondence knowledge and structural analysis to decode words.
3. Reads and comprehends both fiction and nonfiction that is appropriately designed for grade level.
4. Reads longer fictional selections and chapter books independently.
5. Takes part in creative responses to texts such as dramatizations, oral presentations, fantasy play, etc.
6. Can point to or clearly identify specific words or wordings that are causing comprehension difficulties.
7. Summarizes major points from fiction and nonfiction texts.
8. In interpreting fiction, discusses underlying theme or message.

9. Asks how, why, and what-if questions in interpreting nonfiction texts.
10. In interpreting nonfiction, distinguishes cause and effect, fact and opinion, main idea and supporting details.
11. Uses information and reasoning to examine bases of hypotheses and opinions.
12. Infers word meanings from taught roots, prefixes, and suffixes.
13. Correctly spells previously studied words and spelling pattern in own writing.
14. Begins to incorporate literacy words and language patterns in own writing (e.g. elaborates descriptions, uses figurative wording).
15. With some guidance, uses all aspects of the writing process in producing own compositions and reports.
16. Combines information from multiple sources in writing reports.
17. With assistance, suggests and implements editing and revision to clarify and refine own writing.
18. Presents and discusses own writing with other students and responds helpfully to other students' compositions.
19. Independently reviews work for spelling, mechanics, and presentation.
20. Produces a variety of written words (e.g. literature responses, reports, "published" books, semantic maps) in a variety of formats, including multimedia forms.

Accomplishments are reprinted by permission from Catherine E. Snow, M. Susan Burns, and Peg Griffin, eds., *Preventing Reading Difficulties in Young Children* (Washington, D.C.: National Academy Press, 1998).

Phonics Materials

• • •

Evaluating Phonics Based Reading Programs

When you call to request a catalog from any of these phonics based reading programs, be sure to request current research regarding the effectiveness of the program in both clinical and school settings. This is, of course, only a partial listing of available phonics based reading programs. Many of these use a multi-sensory approach and include a variety of audio and video components. Some also provide teacher training programs.

An important aspect of evaluating any phonics program is to determine the match between the phonic generalizations taught and the opportunity students have to use and practice those generalizations in their independent reading. If the phonics program does not come with readers, you will have to provide a wide variety of excellent decodable materials from another source for your children to read. "The types of words which appear in beginning reading texts may well exert a more powerful influence in shaping children's word identification strategies than the method of reading instruction."[1]

Action Reading
PO Box 4944
Cave Creek, AZ 85327
800-378-1046

Alphabetic Phonics
(Texas Scottish Rite Hospital for
    Children, Dyslexia Therapy)
2222 Welborn St.
Dallas, TX 75219-3993
214-559-7885

Chall/Popp Reading Program
(Continental Press)
520 E. Bainbridge
Elizabethtown, PA 17022
800-233-0759

**Discover Intensive Phonics for
    Yourself**
(AGC Software, Inc.)
3471 S. 550 W
Bountiful, Utah 84010
800-333-0054

The Herman Method Institute
Renee Herman
4700 Tyrone Ave.
Sherman Oaks, CA 91423
818-784-9566

Home Quest Learning Labs
(Family Success Associates)
800-767-7409

Jolly Phonics
(AIDC)
PO Box 20
Williston, VT 05495-0020
800-488-2665

Language Tune-Up Kit
(Glencoe Division of McGraw-Hill)
PO Box 543
Blacklick, OH 43004
800-334-7344

**Lindamood-Bell Learning
    Processes**
Pat Lindamood, Nanci Bell
416 Higuera St.
San Luis Obispo, CA 93401
805-541-3836 or 800-233-1819

Merrill Linguistics (K–3)
(SRA Open Court Division of
    McGraw-Hill)
220 East Danieldale Rd.
Desoto, TX 75115
888-772-4543

Modern Curriculum Press
PO Box 2649
Columbus, OH 43216
800-321-3106

Open Court/Breaking the Code
(SRA Open Court Division of McGraw-Hill)
220 East Danieldale Rd.
Desoto, TX 75115
888-772-4543

Orton-Gillingham Academy
PO Box 234
Amenia, NY 12501
914-373-8919

Phonics Pathways and Pyramids
(Rayve Productions)
PO Box 726
Windsor, CA 95492
800-852-4890
Delores Hiskes, publisher
925-449-6983

Phono-Graphix/Read America Inc.
PO Box 1246
Mount Dora, FL 32756
407-332-9144
800-732-3868

Primary Phonics/Explode the Code Language Tool Kit
(Educator's Publishers Service)
31 Smith Place
Cambridge, MA 02138-1089
800-225-5750

Project Read/Language Circle
PO Box 20631
Bloomington, MN 55420
612-884-4880

Reading Center/Dyslexia Institute of Minnesota
1312 7th St. NW
Rochester, MN 55901
507-288-5271

Reading Mastery/Rainbow Edition
(SRA Open Court Division of McGraw-Hill)
220 East Danieldale Rd.
Desoto, TX 75115
888-772-4543

Saxon Phonics
2450 John Saxon Blvd.
Norman, OK 73071
800-284-7019

Sing, Spell, Read, and Write
1000 112th Circle N
Suite 100
St. Petersburg, FL 33716
800-321-8322

Slingerland Institute
One Bellevue Center
411 108th Ave. NE #560
Bellevue, WA 98004
425-453-1190

**The Spalding Education
Foundation**
2814 W. Bell Rd.
Suite 1405
Phoenix, AZ 85053
602-866-7801

Total Reading
PO Box 54465
Los Angeles, CA 90054
800-358-7323

Wilson Language Training
175 West Main St.
Milbury, MA 01527
508-865-5699
Barbara A. Wilson
800-899-8454

Zoo Phonics
PO Box 1219
Groveland, CA 95321
800-622-8104

Books That Repeat Phonetic Elements

• • •

Following is a list of titles in which the phonetic elements (long and short vowel sounds) that children will learn through phonics instruction are repeated in the text. Be aware that any given book in the list may not be completely decodable by your child unless he has received formal instruction in all sound-letter correspondences. However, if you know that one of these sounds is being learned in school, using the recommended books as read-alouds and helping your child to decode the words using the elements he has learned is excellent practice.

Although all of the books included in the reading lists in chapters 3, 4, 5, and 6 were in print and available for purchase through amazon.com or your local bookstore, the titles listed below may not always be available for purchase. They will usually, however, be available for checkout at your public library. The publication dates refer to the original date of publication. In many cases, new editions have been issued.

Short *A*

Flack, Marjorie. *Angus and the Cat*. Doubleday, 1931.

Griffith, Helen. *Alex and the Cat*. Greenwillow, 1982.

Kent, Jack. *The Fat Cat*. Scholastic, 1971.

Most, Bernard. *There's an Ant in Anthony*. William Morrow, 1980.

Nodset, Joan. *Who Took the Farmer's Hat?* Harper and Row, 1985.

Robins, Joan. *Addie Meets Max*. Harper and Row, 1985.

Schmidt, Karen. *The Gingerbread Man*. Scholastic, 1985.

Short and Long *A*

Aliki. *Jack and Jake*. Greenwillow, 1986.

Slobodkina, Esphyr. *Caps for Sale*. Addison-Wesley, 1940.

Short *E*

Ets, Marie Hall. *Elephant in a Well*. Viking, 1972.

Galdone, Paul. *The Little Red Hen*. Scholastic, 1973.

Ness, Evaline. *Yeck Eck*. E. P. Dutton, 1974.

Shecter, Ben. *Hester the Jester*. Harper and Row, 1977.

Thayer, Jane. *I Don't Believe in Elves*. William Morrow, 1975.

Wing, Henry Ritchet. *Ten Pennies for Candy*. Holt, Rinehart and Winston, 1963.

Long *E*

Galdone, Paul. *Little Bo-Peep*. Clarion/Ticknor Fields, 1986.

Keller, Holly. *Ten Sleepy Sheep*. Greenwillow, 1983.

Martin, Bill. *Brown Bear, Brown Bear, What Do You See?* Henry Holt, 1967.

Oppenheim, Joanne. *Have You Seen Trees?* Young Scott Books, 1967.

Soule, Jean. *Never Tease a Weasel*. Parents' Magazine Press, 1964.

Thomas, Patricia. *"Stand Back," said the Elephant, "I'm Going to Sneeze."* Lothrop, Lee and Shepard, 1971.

Short *I*

Browne, Anthony. *Willy the Wimp*. A. A. Knopf, 1984.

Ets, Marie Hall. *Gilberto and the Wind*. Viking, 1966.

Hutchins, Pat. *Titch*. Macmillan, 1971.

Keats, Ezra Jack. *Whistle for Willie*. Viking, 1964.

Lewis, Thomas P. *Call for Mr. Sniff*. Harper and Row, 1981.

Lobel, Arnold. *Small Pig*. Harper and Row, 1969.

McPhail, David. *Fix-It*. E. P. Dutton, 1984.

Patrick, Gloria. *This Is* . . . Carolrhoda, 1970.

Robins, Joan. *My Brother, Will*. Greenwillow, 1986.

Long *I*

Berenstain, Stan and Jan. *The Bike Lesson*. Random House, 1964.

Cameron, John. *If Mice Could Fly*. Atheneum, 1979.

Cole, Sheila. *When the Tide Is Low.* Lothrop, Lee and Shepard, 1985.

Gelman, Rita. *Why Can't I Fly?* Scholastic, 1976.

Hazen, Barbara S. *Tight Times.* Viking, 1979.

Short *O*

Benchley, Nathaniel. *Oscar the Otter.* Harper and Row, 1966.

Dunrea, Olivier. *Mogwogs on the March!* Holiday House, 1985.

Emberley, Barbara. *Drummer Hoff.* Prentice-Hall, 1967.

McKissack, Patricia C. *Flossie & the Fox.* Dial, 1986.

Miller, Patricia, and Ira Seligman. *Big Frogs, Little Frogs.* Holt, Rinehart and Winston, 1963.

Seuss, Dr. *Fox in Socks.* Random House, 1965.

Long *O*

Cole, Brock. *The Giant's Toe.* Farrar, Straus and Giroux, 1986.

Gerstein, Mordicai. *Roll Over!* Crown, 1984.

Johnston, Tony. *The Adventures of Mole and Troll.* G. P. Putnam's Sons, 1972.

————. *Night Noises and Other Mole and Troll Stories.* G. P. Putnam's Sons, 1972.

Shulevitz, Uri. *One Monday Morning.* Charles Scribner's Sons, 1967.

Tresselt, Alvin. *White Snow, Bright Snow.* Lothrop, Lee and Shephard, 1947.

Short *U*

Carroll, Ruth. *Where's the Bunny?* Henry Walck, 1950.

Cooney, Nancy E. *Donald Says Thumbs Down.* G. P. Putnam's Sons, 1987.

Friskey, Margaret. *Seven Little Ducks.* Children's Press, 1940.

Lorenz, Lee. *Big Gus and Little Gus.* Prentice-Hall, 1982.

Marshall, James. *The Cut-Ups.* Viking Kestrel, 1984.

Udry, Janice May. *Thump and Plunk.* Harper and Row, 1981.

Yashima, Taro. *Umbrella.* Viking Penguin, 1958.

Long *U*

Lobel, Anita. *The Troll Music.* Harper and Row, 1966.

Segal, Lore. *Tell Me a Trudy.* Farrar, Straus and Giroux, 1977.

Slobodkin, Louis. *"Excuse Me—Certainly!"* Vanguard Press, 1959.

Books to Enhance
Language Development

• • •

The books listed in this section treat the subject of how children learn to talk. You certainly won't need to read all of them, but browse through one or two; they will give you a great deal of important information that might change the way you talk to your child.

Baron, Naomi S. *Growing Up with Language.* Reading, Mass.: Addison-Wesley, 1992.

A very readable and interesting book with excellent examples of how children learn to use language. After you read some of the amusing stories about children and language, I hope you'll be motivated enough to keep track of all of the wonderful and humorous things your children bring forth in the course of an average day. I found the section about growing up bilingual especially interesting. My daughter and her husband hope to raise bilingual children (English and Japanese) someday, and there are many excellent recommendations that I'll eventually pass along to them.

Fowler, William. *Talking from Infancy: How to Nurture and Cultivate Early Language Development.* Cambridge, Mass.: Brookline Books, 1990. To order, write PO Box 1046, Cambridge, MA 02238-1046 or call 617-868-0360.

This author concludes from his research that "children who receive early language enrichment not only become more proficient in language, but are more competent in other areas as well." If you're feeling a little uneasy about how and when to talk to a baby, this book gives you dozens of practical suggestions.

Healy, Jane M. *Is Your Bed Still There When You Close the Closet Door? How to Have Intelligent and Creative Conversations with Your Kids.* New York: Doubleday, 1992.

Of all the books on the list, this is the one I'd buy if I were still raising kids. Inspired ideas for how to talk to kids. If you get "Duh?" when you ask your child a question, buy this book.

Lansky, Bruce. *Baby Talk: How to Help Your Baby Learn to Talk.* Deep Haven, Minn.: Meadowbrook, 1986.

This compact book is packed with information: games, activities, songs, and rhymes for age levels birth to two plus a language development timetable.

Locke, John L. *The Child's Path to Spoken Language.* Cambridge, Mass.: Harvard University Press, 1993.

This is a scholarly volume for those with more than just a parent's interest in language development. But if you are a curious person who is pursuing this area of interest with a passion, you won't want to overlook this discussion of the topic.

Shaw, Clare. *Talking and Your Child.* London: Headway, 1995.

> Lots of great answers to the questions parents often have about language development.

Wiener, Harvey S. *Talk with Your Child: Using Conversation to Enhance Language Development.* New York: Penguin, 1988.

> Two great aspects of this book include "Eleven Cardinal Rules for Establishing Conversational Families" (shut off the television when the whole family is together and don't talk on the telephone if someone else is present in the room) and the chapter "Chatting at Cribside and Other Tales in the Nursery."

Sources of Epigraphs

• • •

Chapter 1: *I Learned to Read Today*

Strickland Gillian, "The Reading Mother," in *The Best Loved Poems of the American People* (Garden City, N.Y.: Doubleday, 1936), 376.

Chapter 2: *Read It One More Time, Daddy*

Cliff Schimmels, foreword in McEwan, *How to Raise a Reader* (Elgin, Ill.: David C. Cook, 1987), 9.

Chapter 3: *The First Years*

James Russell Lowell, *Books and Libraries and Other Papers* (Boston: Houghton Mifflin, 1871), 9.

Chapter 4: *Off to School*

Emily Dickinson, no. 1263 (c. 1873) in John Bartlett, *Bartlett's Familiar Quotations,* ed. Emily Morison Beck, 14th ed. (Boston: Little, Brown, 1968), 738.

Chapter 5: *The Middle Grades*

C. S. Lewis, "On the Reading of Old Books," in *God in the Dock* (Grand Rapids: Eerdmans), 1983.

Chapter 6: *Books to Entice the Reluctant Reader*

Helen Keller, *The Story of My Life* (Garden City, NY: Doubleday, 1954).

Chapter 7: *Rate Your School's Reading Quotient*

Steven Pinker, quoted in Dianne McGuinness, *Why Our Children Can't Read and What We Can Do about It: A Scientific Revolution in Reading* (New York: Free Press, 1997), ix.

Chapter 8: *Helping Your Child Learn to Read at Home and School*

Sylvia Farnham-Diggory, quoted in Romalda Bishop Spalding and Walter T. Spalding, *The Writing Road to Reading* (New York: William Morrow, 1990), 10.

Chapter 9: *Seventy-Plus Ways to Raise a Reader*

National Academy of Education Commission on Reading, *Becoming a Nation of Readers: The Report of the Commission on Reading* (Washington, D.C.: National Academy of Education, National Institute of Education, Center for the Study of Reading, 1985), 117.

Conclusion

Barry Lopez, *Crow and Weasel* (San Francisco: North Point, 1990), 48.

Notes

• • •

Chapter 1: *I Learned to Read Today*

1. Albert J. Harris and Edward R. Sipay, *Effective Teaching of Reading* (New York: McKay, 1971), 13.

2. Marie Clay, *Becoming Literate* (Portsmouth, N.H.: Heinemann, 1991).

3. Catherine E. Snow, M. Susan Burns, and Peg Griffin, eds., *Preventing Reading Difficulties in Young Children* (Washington, D.C.: National Academy Press, 1998). Bonnie Grossen, "30 Years of Research: What We Now Know about How Children Learn to Read" (Santa Cruz, Calif.: Center for the Future of Teaching and Learning), access at http://www.cftl.org/reading.html

4. Ibid.

5. Marilyn Jager Adams et al., *Phonemic Awareness in Young Children* (Baltimore: Paul H. Brookes, 1998). To order, call 800-638-3775.

6. Beth Ashley, "Rich Parents Less Likely to Read to Kids," *USA Today* (7 November 1996), 1D.

7. Burton J. White, *The First Three Years of Life* (Englewood Cliffs, N.J.: Prentice-Hall, 1975), 111.

Chapter 2: *Read It One More Time, Daddy*

1. Keith Stanovich, "Matthew Effects in Reading: Some Consequences of Individual Differences in the Acquisition of Literacy," *Reading Research Quarterly* 21 (1986): 360–407.

2. Joan Beck, *How to Raise a Brighter Child* (New York: Trident Press, 1967).

Chapter 4: *Off to School*

1. Barbara Barstow and Judith Riggle, *Beyond Picture Books: A Guide to First Readers* (New York: Bowker, 1989).

Chapter 7: *Rate Your School's Reading Quotient*

1. Sybilla Avery-Cook and Cheryl Page, *Books, Battles, and Bees* (New York: American Library Association, 1994). To order, call 800-545-2433.

2. You may wish to visit the following Web site, which contains an analysis of three reading programs used in Fairfax County (Virginia) public schools done by Parents for Improved Education in Fairfax County: http://www.geocities.com/capitolhill/9155/

3. Louisa Cook Moats, "The Missing Foundation in Teacher Education," *American Educator* 9 (summer 1995), 43–51. To request a free copy of this issue, call 202-879-4420 or fax your request to 202-879-4534.

4. Elaine K. McEwan, *The Principal's Guide to Raising Reading Achievement* (Thousand Oaks, Calif.: Corwin Press, 1998).

5. The following section is adapted from McEwan, *The Principal's Guide to Raising Reading Achievement*, with permission from the publisher.

6. Dianne McGuinness, *Why Our Children Can't Read and What We Can Do about It: A Scientific Revolution* (New York: Free Press, 1997), xiii.

7. Linnea C. Ehri, "Sources of Difficulty in Learning to Spell and Read," in *Advances in Developmental and Behavioral Pediatrics*, vol. 7, M. L. Wolraich and D. Routh, eds. (Greenwich, Conn.: JAI, 1986), 121–95.

8. Marilyn Adams, *Beginning to Read: Thinking and Learning about Print* (Cambridge, Mass.: MIT Press, 1990).

9. Barbara Foorman et al., "The Role of Instruction in Learning to Read: Preventing Failure in At Risk Children," *Journal of Educational Psychology* 90 (1998), 37–55.

10. Jerry L. Johns and Susan Davis Lenski, *Improving Reading: A Handbook of Strategies* (Dubuque, Iowa: Kendall/Hunt, 1997).

11. Elaine K. McEwan, *Solving School Problems* (Wheaton, Ill.: Harold Shaw, 1992).

Chapter 8: *Helping Your Child Learn to Read at Home and School*

1. Patrick Groff, *The Reading Competency Test* (The Plains, Va.: The National Right to Read Foundation, 1997).

2. Carmen McGuinness and Geoffrey McGuinness, *Reading Reflex: The Foolproof Phono-Graphix Method for Teaching Your Child to Read* (New York: Free Press, 1998).

3. Albert J. Harris and Edward R. Sipay, *How to Increase Reading Ability* (New York: McKay, 1975).

4. McGuinness and McGuinness, *Reading Reflex*, 45–50.

5. Ibid.

6. Lindamood-Bell Human Learning Management System, *Visualizing and Verbalizing for Language Comprehension and Thinking* (San Luis Obispo, Calif.). This program develops the brain's ability to conceptually image gestalts (wholes) by integrating imagery and language using specific vocabulary to develop and describe components of mental representation.

The Lindamood Phoneme Sequencing (LiPS) Program (San Luis Obispo, Calif.). Increases phonemic awareness. Extensive gains can be expected in word attack, word recognition, contextual reading, and phonetic spelling skills.

Seeing Stars: A Program of Symbol Imagery for Phonemic Awareness, Sight Words, and Spelling (San Luis Obispo, Calif.). Develops the brain's ability to visualize the orthography or symbols used in the English language.

For information on all of the programs, call 800-233-1819.

Chapter 9: *Seventy-Plus Ways to Raise a Reader*

1. Avery-Cook and Page, *Books, Battles, and Bees.*

Resource G: *Phonics Materials*

1. Connie Juel et al., "The Influence of Basals on First Grade Reading," *Reading Research Quarterly* 20 (1985): 137.

References

• • •

Adams, Marilyn. *Beginning to Read: Thinking and Learning about Print.* Cambridge, Mass.: MIT Press, 1990.

Adams, Marilyn Jager, Barbara R. Foorman, Ingvar Lundberg, and Terri Beeler. *Phonemic Awareness in Young Children.* Baltimore: Paul H. Brookes, 1998.

Ames, Louise Bates, and Frances L. Ilg. *Your Five Year Old.* New York: Delacorte, 1979.

———. *Your Four Year Old.* New York: Delacorte, 1976.

———. *Your Six Year Old.* New York: Delacorte, 1979.

Ashley, Beth. "Rich Parents Less Likely to Read to Kids," *USA Today* (7 November 1996), 1D.

Avery-Cook, Sybilla, and Cheryl Page. *Books, Battles, and Bees.* New York: American Library Association, 1994.

Barstow, Barbara, and Judith Riggle. *Beyond Picture Books: A Guide to First Readers.* New York: Bowker, 1989.

Beck, Joan. *How to Raise a Brighter Child.* New York: Trident Press, 1967.

Butler, Dorothy. *Babies Need Books.* New York: Atheneum, 1982.

Butler, Dorothy, and Marie Clay. *Reading Begins at Home.* Exeter, N.H.: Heinemann, 1979.

Chomsky, Carol. "Stages in Language Development and Reading Exposure." *Harvard Educational Review* 42 (1971): 1–33.

Clay, Marie. *Becoming Literate.* Portsmouth, N.H.: Heinemann, 1991.

References

Durkin, Dolores. *Children Who Read Early.* New York: Teachers College Press, 1966.

Ehri, Linnea C. "Sources of Difficulty in Learning to Spell and Read." In *Advances in Developmental and Behavioral Pediatrics,* vol. 7, edited by M. L. Wolraich and D. Routh, 121–95. Greenwich, Conn.: JAI, 1986.

Foorman, Barbara, et al. "The Role of Instruction in Learning to Read: Preventing Failure in At Risk Children." *Journal of Educational Psychology* 90 (1998): 37–55.

Gesell, Arnold L., Frances L. Ilg, and Louise Bates Ames. *The Child from Five to Ten.* New York: Harper and Row, 1946.

Groff, Patrick. *The Reading Competency Test.* The Plains, Va.: The National Right to Read Foundation, 1997.

Grossen, Bonnie. "30 Years of Research: What We Now Know about How Children Learn to Read." Santa Cruz, Calif.: Center for the Future of Teaching and Learning. Access at http://www.cftl.org/reading.html

Harris, Albert J., and Edward R. Sipay. *Effective Teaching of Reading.* New York: McKay, 1971.

———. *How to Increase Reading Ability.* New York: McKay, 1975.

Johns, Jerry L., and Susan Davis Lenski. *Improving Reading: A Handbook of Strategies.* Dubuque, Iowa: Kendall/Hunt, 1997.

Juel, Connie, et al. "The Influence of Basals on First Grade Reading." *Reading Research Quarterly* 20 (1985): 134–52.

Lindamood-Bell Human Learning Management System. *The Lindamood Phoneme Sequencing (LiPS) Program.* San Luis Obispo, Calif.: Lindamood-Bell Human Learning Management System.

———. *Visualizing and Verbalizing for Language Comprehension and Thinking.* San Luis Obispo, Calif.: Lindamood-Bell Human Learning Management System.

———. *Seeing Stars: A Program of Symbol Imagery for Phonemic Awareness, Sight Words, and Spelling.* San Luis Obispo, Calif.: Lindamood-Bell Human Learning Management System.

McEwan, Elaine K. *The Principal's Guide to Raising Reading Achievement.* Thousand Oaks, Calif.: Corwin Press, 1998.

———. *Solving School Problems.* Wheaton, Ill.: Harold Shaw, 1992.

McGuinness, Carmen, and Geoffrey McGuinness. *Reading Reflex: The Foolproof Phono-Graphix Method for Teaching Your Child to Read.* New York: Free Press, 1998.

McGuinness, Dianne. *Why Our Children Can't Read and What We Can Do about It: A Scientific Revolution in Reading.* New York: Free Press, 1997.

Moats, Louisa Cook. "The Missing Foundation in Teacher Education." *American Educator* 9 (Summer 1995): 43–51.

Snow, Catherine E., M. Susan Burns, and Peg Griffin, eds. *Preventing Reading Difficulties in Young Children.* Washington, D.C.: National Academy Press, 1998.

Stanovich, Keith. "Matthew Effects in Reading: Some Consequences of Individual Differences in the Acquisition of Literacy." *Reading Research Quarterly* 21 (1986): 360–407.

Teale, William H. "Positive Environments for Learning to Read: What Studies of Early Readers Tell Us." *Language Arts* 55 (Nov.–Dec. 1978): 922–32.

White, Burton J. *The First Three Years of Life.* Englewood Cliffs, N.J.: Prentice-Hall, 1975.

Wilson, George, and Joyce Moss. *Books for Children to Read Alone: A Guide for Parents and Librarians.* New York: Bowker, 1988.

Subject Index

• • •

Author/Illustrator Index

• • •

Illustrators are in italics

Elaine K. McEwan has been a teacher, school librarian, principal, and assistant superintendent for instruction in the suburban Chicago area. She received her master's degree in library science and Ed.D. in educational administration from Northern Illinois University. She is currently a partner in the McEwan-Adkins Group, a consulting firm offering training in raising reading and math achievement, instructional leadership, and school-community relations.